D1128561

The 50th Anniversary of Wheelchair Basketball

The 50th Anniversary of Wheelchair Basketball

A History by Horst Strohkendl
Editing and Articles by Armand „Tip“ Thiboutot
and Philip Craven

International Wheelchair Basketball Federation

Waxmann
Münster · New York

Die Deutsche Bibliothek – CIP-Einheitsaufnahme

The 50th anniversary of Wheelchair basketball:
a history / Wheelchair Basketball Federation. By Horst Strohkendl. Ed. by Armand „Tip" Thiboutot. – Münster ; New York : Waxmann, 1996
ISBN 3-89325-441-2

NE: Strohkendl, Horst; Thiboutot, Armand [Hrsg.]; International Wheelchair Basketball Federation; The fiftieth anniversary of Wheelchair basketball

ISBN 3-89325-441-2

Postfach 8603, D-48046 Münster, Germany
Waxmann Publishing Co.
P. O. Box 1318, New York, NY 10028, USA

Bookcover and Layout:
Pleßmann Kommunikations Design,
Ascheberg, Germany

Printed by:
Druckerei Runge GmbH,
Cloppenburg, Germany

Contents

Foreword

In 1996 wheelchair basketball can hold its head high and look back on fifty memorable years which have produced a sport that is fast, exciting and a great crowd pleaser.

This sport of ours must be really something special when in the early days it could attract men and women who had to practise in totally inappropriate non sports wheelchairs. But team sports are really special. You are playing together against friends and no matter how hard the game might be, particularly in those early weeks when your hands are covered with blisters, the thrill of participation overcomes all the difficulties.

What an incredible feeling it is when, after all the training, you get into a match situation and know that you have the ability to sink, at will, a fifteen foot shot straight down the throat of the basket. You learn to be in control of your own destiny.

This book recounts major struggles to get our sport off the ground. It also records major achievements and great players who epitomise every aspect of the Olympic ideal.

Horst Strohkendl has dedicated a major part of his life to wheelchair basketball. It is fitting that Horst has masterminded this book's publication and has drawn together many historical sources to give a comprehensive picture of how the sport has grown.

Armand „Tip" Thiboutot editor, of the IWBF's „Basketball News", has once again wielded his red editorial pen in addition to compose certain portions of the text. On this occasion he has transformed Horst's excellent germanically influenced texts into more fluent English prose.

On behalf of all members of the IWBF Executive Committee, I would like to thank all contributors to this book whether this was with the written word or by the effort required to seek out old photographs that may have been stored at the bottom of a trunk in the loft.

So, please enjoy reading the facts about our sport and the achievements of tens of thousands of players and officials who have gained such enjoyment from our sport over the past fifty years. Let's use this book and its shining examples to ensure that millions will thrill to our game over the next fifty years.

Crewe, May 1996

Philip L. Craven MBE
President
International Wheelchair Basketball Federation

Preface

50 years of existence is a relatively short period f the development of wheelchair basketball as sport. However, taking into consideration the li expectation of a person with a spinal cord injury the late 40s, the growth of wheelchair basketb reflects one of the greatest achievements in ma kind. The author of this book has been involved the wheelchair sport movement 27 years no Through his first contact with wheelchair baske ball players in Germany, he experienced a sens tion of great surprise. It was difficult for the auth at that time to equate a person affected by such severe physical disability with one able to play ar enjoy sports. He was inspired and at that time fa cinated to find out more. Could there be a mo exciting challenge to someone who always lov sport and who had learnt from his studies the ed cational values of participation in sport?

It was not difficult to get involved in wheelcha sport at the national and international levels in t late 60s. The „Stoke Mandeville Spirit" touch comparatively few people and inspiration was lin ted mainly to the traditional medical professio Persons with in depth knowledge of and experie ce in the field of sport were hardly visible. T focus at that time was predominantly on rehabilit tion, with sport itself a minor issue. No-one cou have foreseen the tremendous developments th were to occur in the future, not even in the mo speculative of dreams. Nevertheless, the autho ational involvement in 1969 and first international articipation in Stoke Mandeville in 1971 were onderful experiences and opened the door to a ew world of challenges. The marginal situation in hich persons with disabilities in our society found emselves was associated with injustice, prejudice nd lack of fairness. Involvement in wheelchair asketball therefore was always additionally onnected to political issues.

EING A WITNESS throughout the major part of heelchair basketball's history as an eager obser-er and devoted officer of the movement makes it omewhat difficult now to take an impartial and bjective position when writing its history. Even the arginal position of the author, as someone not ffected by a permanent physical impairment, ould be judged as a major disadvantage when riting the history of a sport primarily developed nd played by persons with physical disabilities. If is agreed that a written document cannot always e complete and that words are only simple bstracts of what has been really happening, then he author's position may well turn out to be an dvantage. To think, to discuss and to write have lways been his preferred means of learning about ersons with physical disabilities and their sport. e has tried to understand and to explain what was volving in a way which had no prior comparable odel in the history of rehabilitation. But, in the inal analysis, wheelchair basketball and its players emain for him a mystery of life that has not lost its ascination since his first encounter as a young an.

ACKNOWLEDGEMENT

THE AUTHOR'S APPOINTMENT by the IWBF Executive Committee to work on this project is a great privilege and honour. Having now completed the work, it has proved to be one of the most exciting times of his life. His personal interests faded into the background and he felt profound emotion when he realized that: One serves as a means to write the testimony of wheelchair basketball and its unique contribution in helping to eradicate the discriminatory elements in peoples' relationships that so strongly existed in the past.

IN COMPLETING THIS BOOK, his thanks go to the many people who have contributed and assisted in its production and, in particular, these are addressed to Stan Labanowich who preserved the historical documentation and with whom the author shared the successes over this period of wheelchair basketball's development. Stan Labanowich, as Chairman of the ISMWSF Basketball Section, founded the constitutional base of the IWBF during his time of office from 1973 until 1993.

A MAJOR WORKLOAD in the production of this book has fallen on the shoulders of Armand „Tip" Thiboutot, Vice President of the IWBF since 1988, who has spent uncounted hours in refining and discussing the contents of the text and in correcting the English language. A similar amount of work and assistance has been provided by Philip Craven, President of the IWBF since 1988, who has served most effectively in the capacity of a living resource of history of wheelchair basketball since 1966.

A LIMIT HAS TO BE EXERCISED on the amount of words and phrases required to cover every instance of sorrow, hope, action, defeat and success that have occured over such a lengthy period of time. The author has been in a position to include and record for posterity some of the most important incidences because of his unique relationship to the three persons mentioned above. Endless discussions and hundreds of letters have helped to clarify past developments and allowed him to remain in the mainstream of the evolutionary process.

MANY, MANY PEOPLE have given their support to this project. It would be difficult to try and name them all. Pictures were sent from all over the world, people whom the author had not met before and whose names he did not know had an involvement. The author's sincere thanks are addressed to them all for their contributions.

THE PRODUCTION OF A BOOK obviously requires a financial investment. It was therefore extremely helpful when Wolfgang Raabe of MEYRA indicated his interest. Recognition should also be given to the Department of Special Education at the University of Cologne, Germany whose generous acceptance of a heavy work schedule has meant that the completion of the book has been effected within a six month time frame.

IN CONCLUDING THESE acknowledgements, the author wishes also to give recognition to a major energy resource and what is unfortunately an often underestimated support for expansion within wheelchair basketball. Where would our movement be if wheelchair athletes did not receive support from their families, friends and more importantly, partners? On behalf of the members of the IWBF'Executive-Committee, the author extends most heartful thanks to all the tolerant and wise wives and husbands who support their partners in participating in wheelchair basketball and encourage their successful endeavours as officers of the Federation. They had already demonstrated their belief in a person's integrity and unique value, notwithstanding his/her disability, even before the initial successes of the self-determination movement of wheelchair sport had got off the ground.

Cologne, May 1996

Horst Strohkendl
The author

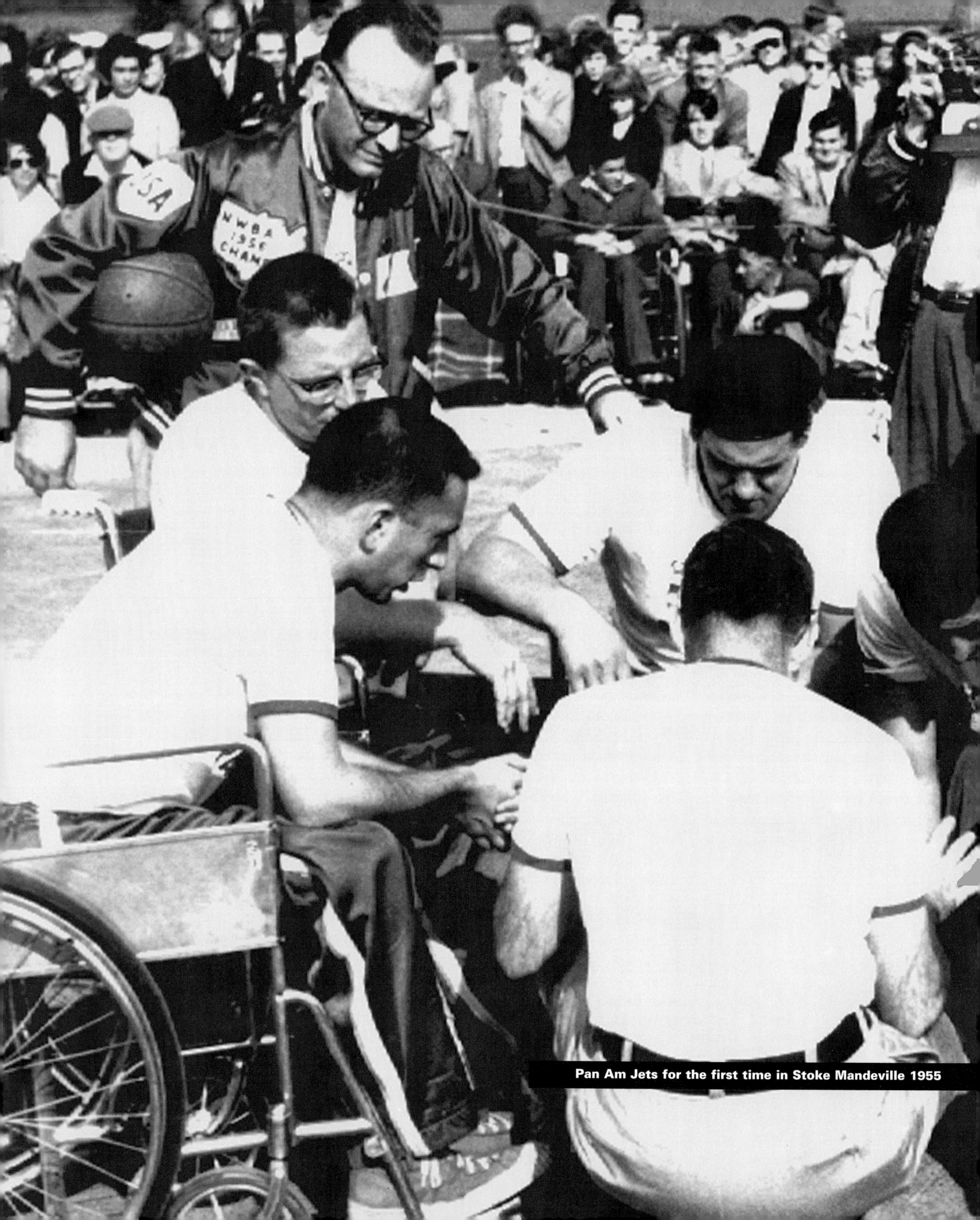

Pan Am Jets for the first time in Stoke Mandeville 1955

Part One

The History of Wheelchair Basketball

There is a strong probability that wheelchair basketball would have been created by wheelchair players,...

...EVEN IF THE RUNNING BASKETBALL MODEL HAD NOT PRECEDED IT. THE BASIC PRINCIPLES OF THE GAME OF BASKETBALL FIT IDEALLY WITH THE FUNCTIONAL ABILITIES OF PERSONS USING SELF-PROPELLED WHEELCHAIRS.

LOOKING BACK into the history of sports for persons with disabilities, especially those using wheelchairs, no one today could imagine the difficulties that the pioneers faced. The foundation of rehabilitation as a medical discipline is one of the major achievments of this century, but it did not necessarily include the promotion of sports for persons with disabilities. Even today, sports programmes are only included in a small number of hospitals and they are normally organized in conjunction with the treatment of spinal cord injuries. Only exceptionally motivated people who found themselves in the right place at the right time could help develop and promote the first efforts initiated by persons with disabilities.

WHEELCHAIR SPORTS and wheelchair basketball started to develop almost at the same time in the US and the United Kingdom around the end of the World War II. This is a history of wheelchair basketball, which is no ordinary sport, but an exciting success story, a narrative depicting athletic achievement and admirable human values.

THE AMERICAN BRANCH OF WHEELCHAIR BASKETBALL

ACCORDING TO ONE of the earliest recorders of the game, the devoted administrator of the Paralysed Veterans of America (PVA) and one of the early Presidents of the National Wheelchair Basketball Association (NWBA), Harry A. Schweikert Jr., wheelchair basketball emerged both on the west and the east coasts of the United States of America in the year 1946 (SCHWEIKERT 1954, CRASE 1982). The wards of the Veterans Administration Hospitals were full of young men with spinal cord injuries, casualties of the greatest tragedy thus far in the history of mankind, World War II. Only a short time before, in Great Britain in 1944, Sir Ludwig Guttmann succeeded in developing a treatment method that prevented spinal cord injured individuals from succumbing to life threatening secondary complications such as pressure sores and kidney infections (GUTTMANN 1976, 22). Disciplined full time care and special training could give persons with spinal cord injuries a full-life expectancy. Complete paralysis of the sensory and motor functions of the body below the site of the spinal cord injury meant that a wheelchair was the only device that would allow independent mobility.The Everest and Jennings folding wheelchair, invented in 1932, was the chair made available to young and active war veterans.

WARD 505

	Goals	Fouls	Points
M. Leonard rf	0	0	0
R. Foley lf.........	2	0	4
N. Lehnowsky c....	2	0	4
R. Abelson rb......	3	0	6
W. Bozek lb........	0	0	0
Totals............	7	0	14

WARD 507

	Goals	Fouls	Points
D. Pinault lb......	0	0	0
L. Drew rb.........	0	0	0
W. Maguire c......	6	0	12
G. Seymourian lf..	0	0	0
E. McLeod rf......	0	0	0
Totals............	6	0	12

Referee, R. Laramie.

Wheelchair Basketball's first recorded scoresheet

New England Clippers (1947) at Cushing VAH, Framingham, Massachusetts

HE DEVELOPMENT of wheechair basketball is related
the unaffected desire to live which still burned in
any young individuals (approx. 2500 war veter-
ns with spinal cord injuries in the US), who regar-
ed themselves as their country's heroes. They
ought entertainment and excitement instead of
oring hospital life, where the idea of being *confi-
ed* to a wheelchair often signified misery in its
orst form. Anyone using calipers or prostheses
as regarded as much less disabled and less tor-
ented, even by the wheelchair users themselves.
e cannot admire enough those individuals who
vercame all the prejudices and psychological limi-
ations of the 1940s. How strange must have been
he idea to medically trained personnel that some-
ody in a wheelchair would play sports, sports
hich seemed to be the exclusive privilege of
oung, physically talented and non-disabled per-
ons.

HEELCHAIR BASKETBALL TOURNAMENTS and demonstra-
ion events were organized from 1946 on by the
aralyzed Veterans of America (PVA), when most
araplegics in other countries still suffered and
ied in hospital beds totally isolated from the
ublic. Patricia Thiboutot, of Boston, has found
ocumentation in the „Framingham News" (MA),
that disabled veterans of World War II who were
hen hospitalized at the Cushing Veterans Admini-
tration Hospital in Framingham played and defea-
ed the Boston Celtics 18 - 2 on December 6, 1946.
subsequent article, published in the same news-
aper on February 21, 1947, describes a game in
hich ward 505 of Cushing Hospital defeated ward
07 by two points, 14 - 12" (THIBOUTOT 1995,
4). Harry A Schweikert Jr. reports on a demon-
tration event in Madison Square Garden, New York
n the 10th March 1948, when 15,561 spectators
heered the teams from Cushing Hospital Framing-
am, later called the New England Clippers, and the
alloran Hospital located in New York. The well-
nown national news magazine *Newsweek* (Vol.
XXI, No. 12, March 22, 1948), displayed a photo

St. Albans US Navy Hospital PVA Halloran Vets Hospital, 1940s

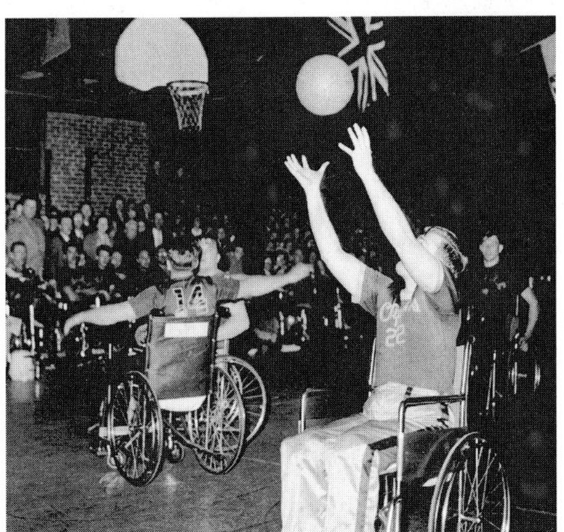

Flying Wheels from California in Cushing Hospital, Feb. 1948 Cushing – California 18:6

Jack Gerhardt, Newsweek magazine, March 22, 1948

of a player, Jack Gerhardt, on its front page and reported on an exciting game of wheelchair basketball. The Halloran Team won 20 to 11.

ONE YEAR BEFORE the introduction of the Birmingham PVA Chapter team, *the Flying Wheels* of California, toured the US by plane. The New England Clippers, defeated the Flying Wheels 18 - 6. That tour contributed significantly to the recognition of the new sport. In 1948, the PVA awarded a championship trophy to the team that had obtained the best record of all matches played between the teams

...ing Pioneers Win Wheelchair Meet

...ty Team Halts ...is Win Streak; ...op Third Place

TO THE VICTORS went the trophies when the National Wheelchair Basketball tournament ended at the Galesburg armory last night. Pictured above, from left to right, are Larry Swanson, captain of the Minneapolis Rolling Gophers, second place winners; Shirley Sayers, cheerleader of the Gizz Kids of the Galesburg division of the University of Illinois, who made the presentations; Bob Miller, captain of the championship Rolling Pioneers of Kansas City, Mo.; and Don Swift, captain of the Gizz Kids, winners of third place in the tournament.

Stellar Lineup Meets 'Rollers'

8 Duluth News-Tribune, Sunday, March 6, 1949.

'Rolling Gophers' to Exhibit Cage Technique Here Next Sunday

Wheelchair Tilt Scheduled

One of the most novel basketball teams in the nation "rolls" into Duluth next Sunday to give cage fans something new in the way of court entertainment at the Duluth armory.

They are the "Rolling Gophers," a group of wheelchair patients whose love for sports has carried them from the role of spectators into actual competition despite their physical handicaps.

The "Rolling Gophers" have won national prominence with their wheelchair basketball game.

They are coached by Eldon Pederson, now on leave from Huron college, Huron, S. D., where he has been athletic director and cage mentor for the last three years.

Players range in age from 18 to 30 years and include disabled World war II veterans.

Opposing them will be players from the University of Minnesota, Duluth branch, who also will play from wheelchairs.

from the PVA hospitals located throughout the USA. The teams were ranked by an independent jury from the Helms Foundation in Los Angeles. The common denominator of all PVA teams was that all players were paraplegics. This kind of competition and ranking lasted until 1951 (LABANOWICH 1975, 33f.).

WHEELCHAIR BASKETBALL at that time hardly resembled today's game. This sport did not have nationally accepted rules and regulations. Each team offered its own interpretations on the rules. Most matches did not start before there were lengthy discussions on rules, which could not always be agreed upon to the satisfaction of both teams. This difficulty became almost volatile, when the Kansas City Bulldozers, later called the Rolling Pioneers even allowed intentional charging with their wheelchairs (LABANOWICH 1975, 34). This was understandable for individuals who looked to wheelchair basketball as an outlet for their pent up aggression and frustration. In the US during the early years, wheelchair basketball resembled a mixture of basketball and American football

BECAUSE THE TEAMS LIVED far away from each other, it was not uncommon to play against non-disabled friends using wheelchairs. It is unlikely that such an experience which was also reported by the first team from Quebec/Canada in 1951, *the Wheelchair Wonders*, could have occurred in Europe. For a long time, the idea of sitting in a wheelchair was almost regarded as blasphemous by non-disabled persons.

A MAJOR CHANGE CAME with the establishment of hometown teams. Players with physical disabilities other than paraplegia joined this exciting sport. Their disabilities included polio and leg amputations. The paraplegics found themselves in a minority on court and a short time afterwards on the team roster as well. This experience generated questions focusing on classification and fair participation for all players.

IN ADDITION, THE PROBLEM of amateur versus professional status was identified by Harry Schweikert. He regarded the hometown teams as professionals because of their fundraising efforts and because exhibition games were frequently played to raise funds (SCHWEIKERT 1949,8). The PVA complained about this development, because the focus on competition and exhibition was not accompanied by equal efforts in recruiting new players and teams. The old problems remain current ones. Players tend to preserve the sport for themselves rather than encourage new players. This leads to aging teams.

THE RIGHT PLACE and the right time were synchronized for Timothy Nugent to enter on to the wheelchair basketball scene. With his overflowing energy and optimism, he provided the pedagogic supplement to the medical work of Sir Ludwig Guttmann. The latter had the vision and formulated the *Utopia* promising the integration of persons with disabilities into society. Nugent provided the necessary and essential means to achieve this noble goal. True to his philosophy, he organized on the 1st, 2nd and 3rd April 1949 in Galesburg, Illinois, the National

Tim Nugent at Champaign-Urbana Illinois, USA, the complement to Sir Ludwig Guttmann and Stoke Mandeville

heelchair Basketball Association (NWBA). His sic priniciples in rehabilitation of persons with sabilities read as follows (NUGENT 1964, 33f.):

> What a person can achieve, can only be measured by how far you challenge him or her.
> A disability is not necessarily a disaster but a challenge of life. An individual who overcomes his/her disability grows as a person.
> Persons with disabilities have the right to develop their own identity by means of trial and error. The non-disabled can assist, but only to provide a stage for this important experience.

E CONSTITUTION OF THE NWBA follows Nugent's basic emocratic concept: it allows a maximum of player volvement and contribution. The national chamonships were and continue to be held in conjunc- on with the annual general meeting of the teams, e legislative body of the NWBA. Only players ould hold the four, later five, positions on the Exe- tive Committee (LABANOWICH 1975, 62). ugent served the NWBA as Technical Advisor and ommissioner. He was the real driving force from 949 until 1973, but he had no voting rights. He garded persons with disabilities as the real perts in rehabilitation, individuals who live, ink, suffer, enjoy and experience limitations as ell as opportunities twenty-four hours a day. What unique and clear concept, one which nobody nderstood in the world of medical rehabilitation that time. He demonstrated the value of his phi- sophy at the University of Illinois in Champaign- rbana. Wheelchair basketball served as his most fective and convincing model. Timothy Nugent's contribution to the development of rehabilitation of persons with disabilities was appropriately recognized when he received the National Rehabilitation Association's W.F. Faulkes Award on 22nd Oct. 1968.

IN 1973, NUGENT RETIRED as Commissioner of the NWBA. As a result of his influence, wheelchair basketball in the US was established as an effective democratic and player-oriented organization. The sport was administered by commonly accepted rules and regulations. A classification system was established in 1965. Since 1949, the highlight of each NWBA year has been the championship tournament and the annual general meeting of the teams' representatives who discuss and vote on all issues involving the association and elect the officers of the executive committee. Tim Nugent was succeeded by his devoted student, Stan Labanowich. Many of the achievements of international wheelchair basketball and especially that of the IWBF were based on the philosophy of self-determination which, in the field involving the rehabilitation of paraplegics, was first defined by Nugent.

STAN LABANOWICH BEGAN his first-hand experience in international wheelchair sports as a coach and escort of the US team in 1963. He promoted Nugent's concept of rehabilitation and sports in the international arena and became a passionate advocate of democracy. But it was not easy to convince the international community, especially the leaders in Stoke Mandeville, of the value of Nugent's revolutionary concepts in rehabilitation and sports for persons who have disabilities. In the face of Sir Ludwig Guttmann's autocratic leadership, as well as the common attitude of medical specialists and staff who continued to regard disabled athletes as patients, Labanowich found few collaborators in the 1960s and early 1970s. However, he continued to fight for the recognition of democratic principles in the governance of wheelchair basketball.

Stan Labanowich as coach of the famous Illinois Gizz Kids. Players from left: Jim Taylor, Ed Owen, Kim Pollock, Tom Brown and Joe Arcese

The English branch of wheelchair basketball

Many people in the world believe that wheelchair basketball originated in Stoke Mandeville/Aylesbury, England. There is no doubt, that wheelchair sports such as archery, table tennis, javelin throwing were first practiced at that famous place, where the modern treatment for spinal cord injuries was developed by Sir Ludwig Guttmann in the year 1944. Actually, the first team sport played at this first Spinal Injuries Centre in Britain established at Stoke Mandeville Hospital was wheelchair polo, which was later replaced by netball in 1947, a distant „cousin" of basketball. The two baskets had no backboard, and were free-standing at each end of the court. There was no dribbling rule; the ball was merely passed between players. There were no time regulations, except two halves of 15 minutes duration. Each basket counted only one point. This kind of game was played till 1955 in Stoke Mandeville (LABANOWICH & THIBOUTOT 1991, 49). The foldable Everest and Jennings wheelchair was unknown in Stoke Mandeville in the 1940s. The players used heavy armchairs with front wheel propulsion. They proved difficult to steer and frequently caused involuntary spins when trying to move at high speed.

Sir Ludwig Guttmann, devoted physician and successful promoter of wheelcair sports worldwide

First woman playing wheelchair netball in Stoke Mandeville, 1949

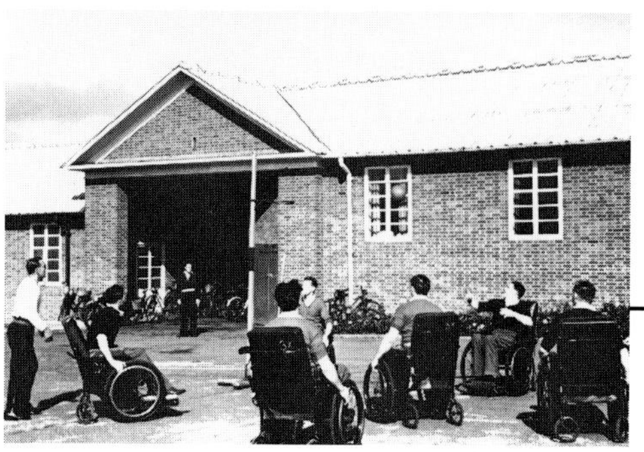

Heavy wheelchairs, 50kg and difficult to push straight Stoke Mandeville in 1949

Wheelchair Polo, the first team sport in Stoke Mandeville, 1946

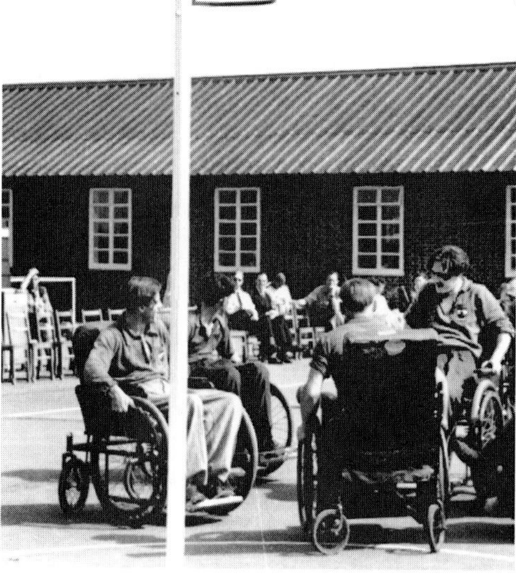

Wheelchair netball, first time introduced into the programme of Stoke Mandeville Games in 1949

The patients at Stoke Mandeville enjoyed their activities, which had been initiated by medical personnel. However, the potential of spinal cord injured people was unintentionally underrated. Medical professionals and staff naturally focused primari the severe disabling effect of their patients' han-caps. The time when players were to be promo-d as athletes was relagated to the future.

VERTHELESS, the international wheelchair basket-ll community owes the International Stoke Man-ville movement a great debt for the extraordina-ly swift world-wide dissemination of new treat-ent methods for spinal cord injuries, and subse-ently for wheelchair sports programmes as a eans of therapy and rehabilitation. Devoted doc-rs visited Stoke Mandeville to study the treatment spinal cord injuries. Having been inspired by the oke *Mandeville Spirit*, they looked forward to turning to Stoke with a team to participate in the nual Games (GUTTMANN 1976). Sir Ludwig Gutt-ann and many medical doctors have been critici-d for their attitude of overprotection and patro-zation of persons with severe physical disabilities (CRAVEN 1989, THIBOUTOT 1990), but their promotion of sporting activities amongst persons with spinal paralysis was a totally new concept in medical care and rehabilitation. This contribution is magnified by the fact that similar programmes did not exist for people with other disabilities.

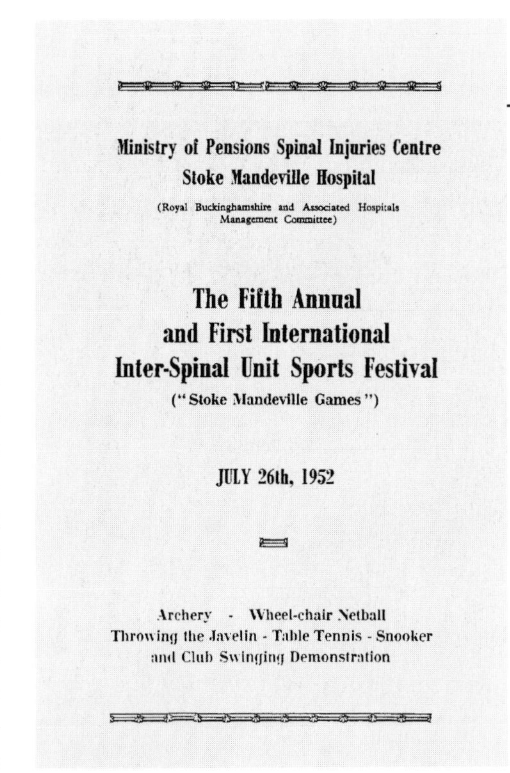

Ministry of Pensions Spinal Injuries Centre
Stoke Mandeville Hospital
(Royal Buckinghamshire and Associated Hospitals Management Committee)

The Fifth Annual
and First International
Inter-Spinal Unit Sports Festival
("Stoke Mandeville Games")

JULY 26th, 1952

Archery - Wheel-chair Netball
Throwing the Javelin - Table Tennis - Snooker
and Club Swinging Demonstration

Programme of the „First International Games" in Stoke Mandeville 1952

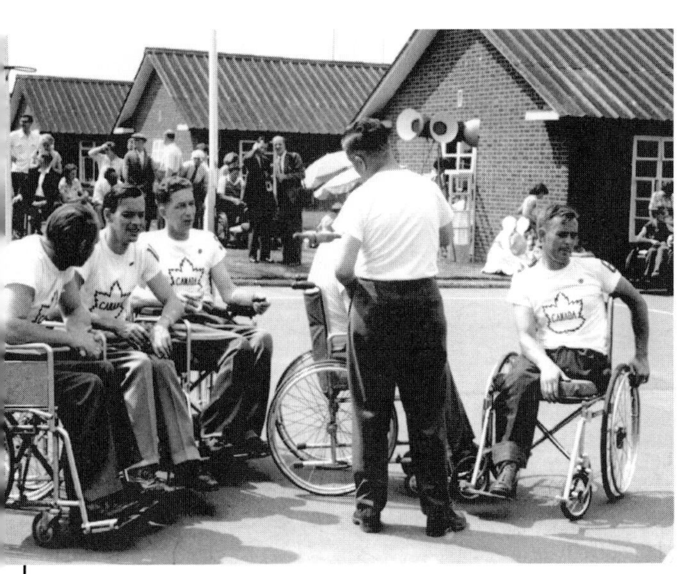

First participants from North America, „Les Wheelchair Wonders" from Quebec, Canada in Stoke Mandeville 1953

INDEED SIR LUDWIG GUTTMANN'S missionary attitude, inspired by his initial experiences in physical rehabilitation, also focused on attitudinal changes in society. He wanted to demonstrate that individuals with spinal cord injuries, „confined to a wheelchair", could achieve and enjoy a meaningful life. He tried to accomplish this major task through devotion, the only way he was equipped to reach the goal he had set for himself and his patients. He was first and foremost a medical doctor who felt that his decisions should be obeyed. He was not a pedagogue and was unfamiliar with democratic procedures. Without autocratic leadership and extreme discipline, he may not have been successful in keeping spinal cord injured people alive.

ON THE 27TH JULY 1948, the date of the opening ceremony of the Olympic Games in London, Sir Ludwig Guttmann organized the first Stoke Mandeville Games. He perceived, in a visionary manner, the inclusion of wheelchair sports, for men and women with spinal cord injuries, into the Olympic Games. It was an inspirational idea, a belief in man's unlimited resources and creativity, conceived only a few years after the genocide of the Jewish people, to whom he belonged. In fact, he viewed the ideal of actual integration of wheelchair sports into the Olympic movement as the measure of the rate of acceptance and integration of persons using wheelchairs by society at large.

IN 1952, THE Stoke Mandeville Games were called international due to the fact that veterans from the Netherlands participated for the first time. During subsequent years, many European countries joined the movement. In 1953, a team from Canada, the Wheelchair Wonders of Quebec, became the first wheelchair basketball team from North America to participate at the second International Stoke Mandeville Games. The news about the *Mecca* for wheelchair sports was beginning to reach the entire world.

THE AMERICAN BRANCH and the English branch came together for the first time in 1955, when the USA's Pan Am Jets appeared at Stoke Mandeville on their

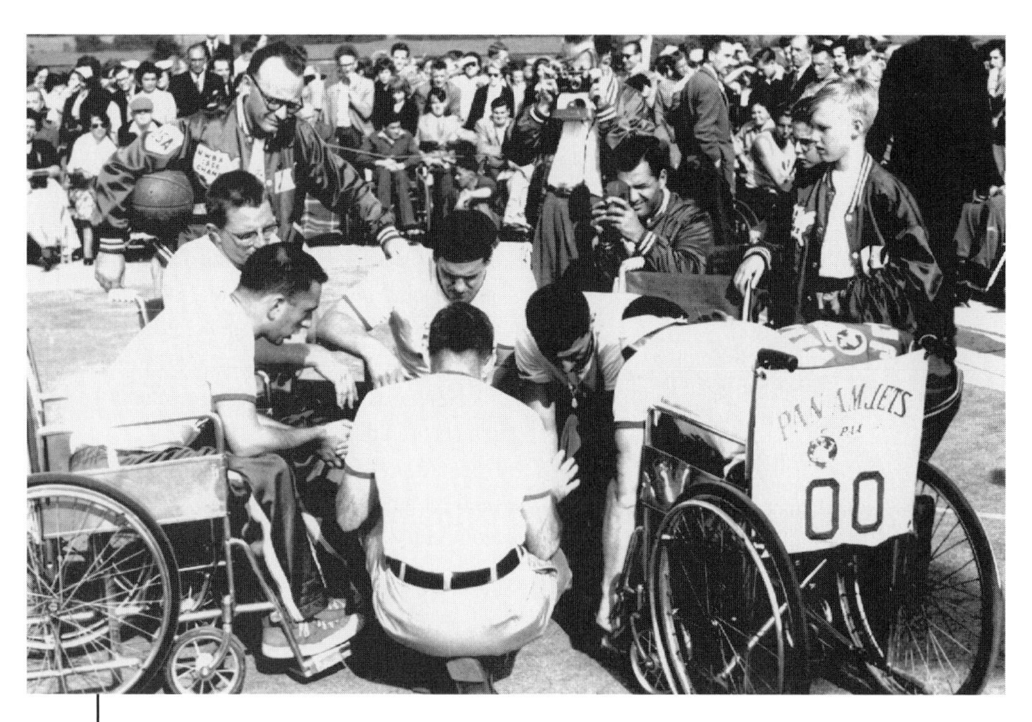

Pan Am Jets for the first time in Stoke Mandeville 1955

world tour (LABANOWICH 1987). What a surprise it must have been for them, after having experienced the well-established basketball competitions of the NWBA in the USA, to play netball in a car park. The Pan Am Jets demonstrated superior wheelchair and ball skills in defeating the British team from Lyme Green Settlement 14 to 7 (a basket counted 1 point), the Dutch team 11 to 2 and a second English team from Duchess of Gloucester House 21 to 3. Unfortunately, the all-conquering Jets, who continued to enjoy competing at Stoke Mandeville in the following years, were disqualified in 1957 by Sir Ludwig because of what he considered rough play (LABANOWICH 1987).

THIS FARCICAL SITUATION signalled a major problem for the future development of wheelchair sports and, in particular, wheelchair basketball. On the one hand, the patronizing attitude of medical professionals underestimated the actual potential of the athletes, whilst on the other hand, the athletes only thought sport and not disability. In the USA this conflict was resolved when in 1951, the PVA stopped awarding its championship trophy to the Veterans Administration Hospital teams. In Stoke Mandeville this problem was only resolved after Sir Ludwig Guttmann had passed away, early in 1980.

SIR LUDWIG'S PATRONIZING attitude was copied by his collaborators in the establishment of wheelchair sports. Such an attitude led to the exclusion of athletes with disabilities other than paralysis from ISMGF wheelchair sports programmes and to the differentiation in international wheelchair basketball between complete and incomplete lesions, in other words teams consisting of players with complete spinal cord injuries who were more disable[d] and teams consisting of players with incomple[te] spinal cord injuries who were less disabled. It to[ok] pressure from participating countries to chan[ge] from netball to wheelchair basketball and to insi[st] on the rules being based as closely as possible o[n] those of FIBA. Andre Auberger reports about suc[h] endeavours by the French team in 1957 (FEDERATION FRANCAISE HANDISPORT). Special recognition was given to both French referees, Mr. Boub[e] and Mr. Bossion, by Sir Ludwig Guttmann (ANONYMOUS 1957 & 1958). In the future, greater emphasis was to be given to the recruitment of refere[es] from running basketball. The member countries [of] the ISMGF were encouraged and asked to inclu[de] basketball referees into their teams when attendin[g] the annual World Wheelchair Games.

2nd Paralympic tournament in Tokyo 1964: Israel v Japan

André Raes, Belgium, first Chairman of the Wheelchair Basketball Section of the ISMGF and outstanding promoter in the field of sports for the disabled

TERNATIONAL RECOGNITION of wheelchair sports was ghlighted when Sir Ludwig Guttmann was awar-d the Fearnley Cup in 1956 by the International ympic Committee (IOC) (GUTTMANN 1976, 33). en in 1960, the first Paralympic Games took pla- two weeks after the regular Olympiad in Rome. heelchair basketball for men was played in two parate competitions, one for complete and one r the more physically able incomplete pla-rs at the next Paralympics in Tokyo in 1964. e US teams won both Gold medals in Rome d Tokyo. The fact that players with polio ere generally physically superior to spinal rd injured players was criticized by no one, d especially not by the spinal cord injured hletes themselves.

FORTUNATELY, THE LEADERS of wheelchair bas-tball failed to acknowledge the physical abi-ies of athletes until 1968, when the Medical mmittee of the International Stoke Mandeville mes Federation (ISMGF) designed a classifica-n system for the amalgamation of complete and complete classes/teams. It was thought that a ree class/12 points system per team would gua-ntee the participation of paraplegics with com-ete thoracic lesions, originating at T10 and abo-. The players and coaches soon discovered the eaknesses of the system, which was applied sole- on a therapy table, away from the court, and had effective control criteria. The players with complete lesions, mostly persons with polio, abu-d the system to their advantage leaving the pla-rs with complete spinal cord injuries, especially ose with high thoracic lesions, on the sideline d very upset. Complaints were ignored because e medical people in charge were unable to provi- better medical solutions.

IS CONFLICT WITHIN THE 1968 classification system ndered the inclusion of other disabilities such as nputees. Participation of paraplegics was already reatened by the players with polio. The view held by the medical personnel was that the inclusion of other disabilities would increase the problems in classification and reduce the number of paraplegics even further. This policy was maintained at Stoke Mandeville, even though it was known that in most countries players with many different physical disabilities were being included in wheelchair basketball programmes.

2nd Commonwealth Games in Kingston, Jamaica in 1966: Australian Team

SOME WHEELCHAIR BASKETBALL events scheduled away from Stoke Mandeville helped prepare a more receptive environment for wheelchair basketball related issues. In 1962 the first British Commonwealth Multi-Sport Games were organized in Perth, Australia. Four years later, Sir John Golding succeeded in staging the second Games in the exotic country of Jamaica. In 1967, the first Pan Am Multi-Sport Games took place in Winnipeg/Manitoba, Canada, including for the first time players with disabilities other than spinal cord injuries on the international scene. In 1970 André Raes organized the first European Wheelchair Basketball Championships in Bruges, Belgium, which were followed the next year by the second European Championships in Kerpape, France and the 1st Gold Cup in 1973, again organized by André Raes in Bruges, Belgium.

1st Gold Cup Tournament in Bruges, Belgium 1973: from left Sir Ludwig Guttmann, Bob Deruelle, Belgium (designed the Gold Cup Logo) and the Captain of the GB-team

Reuven Heller, Isreal, devoted promoter of wheelchair sports both on national and international level

FINALLY IN 1973, Guttmann agreed to the establishment of the then entitled Sub-Section for Wheelchair Basketball within the ISMGF. Even though the 3 officers were elected by 17 representatives of wheelchair basketball playing countries, (André Raes (Chairman), Kenneth Hart, (G.B.) and Stan Labanowich, (USA), they were controlled by the Executive Committee, Technical Committee and Medical Committee of the ISMGF. The officers of the latter committees were not elected, but appointed by Sir Ludwig Guttmann. At last, a first and important step had been made to revitalize wheelchair basketball world-wide as a player-oriented organization focusing on Nugent's philosophy of self-determination. It must be noted at this point that self-determination is present in all wheelchair basketball players. It was not invented by Nugent, only noticed, defined and encouraged.

Closing ceremony with Gold Cup flag at 1st Gold Cup in Bruges 1973

The Resolution towards Self-determination

THE EXECUTIVE COMMITTEE of the ISMGF accepted with reluctance the implementation of the Sub-Section for Wheelchair Basketball in 1973. From a constitutional point of view, it was no more than an organizing committee for the basketball programme at the annual Stoke Mandeville Games. The major decisions, negotiations for and representations of the Federation at major wheelchair basketball tournaments were made by Sir Ludwig Guttmann and his staff members.

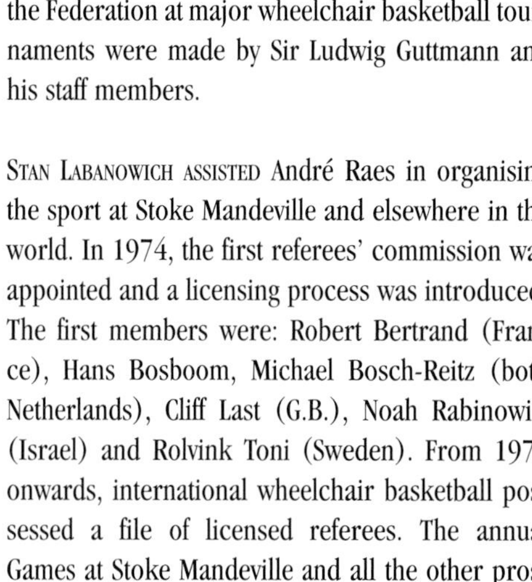

STAN LABANOWICH ASSISTED André Raes in organising the sport at Stoke Mandeville and elsewhere in the world. In 1974, the first referees' commission was appointed and a licensing process was introduced. The first members were: Robert Bertrand (France), Hans Bosboom, Michael Bosch-Reitz (both Netherlands), Cliff Last (G.B.), Noah Rabinowitz (Israel) and Rolvink Toni (Sweden). From 1975 onwards, international wheelchair basketball possessed a file of licensed referees. The annual Games at Stoke Mandeville and all the other prospective international tournaments were used as the sites for productive meetings of the Sub-Section for Wheelchair Basketball, as well as for the adoption of rules and regulations on a democratic basis.

Stan Labanowich, 2nd Chairman Wheelchair Basketball Section of the ISMGF (1976 - 1988)

IN 1976, ELECTIONS took place for the three office of the Sub-Section for Wheelchair Basketball. Sta Labanowich became Chairman. Reuven Heller Israel and Horst Strohkendl of Germany were als elected. André Raes concentrated on the organiza tion of the Gold Cup tournaments. He presided ove the Gold Cup Committee, which could look bac with pride on two superbly organized tourna ments in 1973 (8 European teams participated and in 1975, with teams representing the enti world of wheelchair basketball. Stan Labanowic and his Committee continued to solidify the organ sation by improving the conduct and administrat on of wheelchair basketball tournaments such a the 5th Paralympics in Toronto 1976, the 4th Eur pean Wheelchair Basketball Championships Raalte, Holland in 1977, the 5th European Chan pionships in Lorient, France in 1978 and the thir Gold Cup in Tampa, Florida in 1979. His Commi tee had recognizable support from the basketba playing ISMGF member country organisations, b was observed with some suspicion by the oth Committees within ISMGF. The inner structure the Sub-Section for Wheelchair Basketball wa organised according to the model established the NWBA in the US. Unfortunately, at that time pla yers were not yet very influential at internationa level and did not serve on the Sub-Section f Wheelchair Basketball. The few players who trie challenge the power of the governing authorities ecame increasingly frustrated and were even banned from the movement by Sir Ludwig Guttmann. ne only way to change the promotion of heelchair basketball to a player-oriented sports ovement was to focus on improving the quality of e conduct of this new sport and its presentation the public.

HEELCHAIR BASKETBALL established itself as the most xciting wheelchair sport. Final matches of the urnament proved to be the highlight of the nnual Stoke Mandeville World Games, an eye-cater for the growing number of wheelchair basketall enthusiasts in Aylesbury and in many other plaes throughout the world.

AN LABANOWICH DEMONSTRATED strong leadership and e Sub-Section members supported him consisntly. Wheelchair Basketball became the leading rce for all other sports. However, it still did not ave sufficient power to promote change. Labanoich was most frustrated when he realized that the rganizing Committee for the 6th Paralympics in rnhem in 1980 was not even aware of the existen- of the Sub-Section for Wheelchair Basketball. he actual negotiations were still conducted by the chnical Committee of the ISMGF. After negotiaons with the authorities in Arnhem, Labanowich as accepted as the Technical Delegate, one who ould ensure the proper conduct of the Paralympic ournament. The Technical Committee of the MGF had no influence at all at the Basketball ournament in Arnhem. The international wheelhair basketball community felt stronger and focued with greater intensity on its own affairs. The rganizational structure of the ISMGF did not meet e actual needs of the sport. The time for change ad arrived.

T THE MEETINGS HELD in conjunction with the Arnhem aralympics, a dialogue was started with represenatives from the Netherlands, a dialogue that focused on the inclusion of players with amputations at the international level. These meetings also resulted in encouraging wheelchair basketball playing countries to seek affiliation with their non-disabled counterparts in FIBA. A new Executive Committee of the Sub-Section consisting of five members was elected. Sub-committees for officiating, rules and competitions were established. The number of actively involved individuals serving the Sub-Section for Wheelchair Basketball was significantly increased.

THE 1981 EUROPEAN Wheelchair Basketball Championships were held in Geneva, Switzerland. The ISMGF authorities again sanctioned an external organizing committee, this time in Geneva, a committee which had no affiliation to the governing authorities of wheelchair sports in Switzerland; it possessed only scant knowledge of the standards expected in conducting the European Championships. Consequently, the opening and closing ceremonies were given more recognition than the matches. Players and officials were accommodated in nuclear fallout bunkers. It was obvious that the presence of the players and the teams primarily served the purposes of the tournament's interest groups, who really had their own agendas.

THE COMPETENCE AND AUTHORITY of the ISMGF were challenged. The major issue, inclusion of players with other disabilities, was discussed by the team representatives. The so-called „paraplegic countries“ expressed great concern at the prospect of including other disabilities under the present classification system. Horst Strohkendl of Germany briefly informed the delegates that a more suitable classification system, a player-oriented functional system for wheelchair basketball was available, which could remedy the existing problems and also include players with other disabilities. The Executive Committee was mandated to conduct an in-depth investigation that would hopefully resolve this controversy.

IN 1981 THE ISMGF formulated its first Constitution under a new President, Dr. Robert Jackson of Canada, giving all sports permission to form their own sub-sections. The planned ratification of the new Constitution at the council meeting in 1982 in Stoke Mandeville shifted the legislative power away from the traditional leadership in Stoke Mandeville to the member countries of the ISMGF. This shift in power also coincided with the application by the Sub-Section for Wheelchair Basketball to include other disabilities into international wheelchair basketball competitions.

BUT BEFORE PLAYERS and advocates of wheelchair basketball could hope for the adoption of their proposal by the delegates of the ISMGF member countries, the classification problem had to be solved as well. During the superbly conducted European Wheelchair Basketball Championships in Falun, Sweden in 1982, the Sub-Section formed its own Classification Committee. Stan Labanowich was challenged by Philip Craven, a player on the British team, who complained about ongoing abuses in classification and the unfairness they constituted not only for certain teams, but also for players with thoracic lesions. After learning about the inactivity of the Medical Committee and its obvious reluctance to accept a player-oriented functional classification system, one which had for years been ready for implementation, the wheelchair basketball authorities, adviced by Stan Labanowich, had to take this important task into their own hands. Dr. Cairbre McCann of the USA, the new Chairman of the Medical Committee (ISMGF), who at first seemed to support an improved classification system, but was not prepared to accept a functional and player-oriented system which was challenging the hitherto exclusive authority of the medical profession to formulate classification systems within the wheelchair sport movement.

THE FIRST sport specific classification committee was formed in Falun with Horst Strohkendl as Chairman and with members Philip Craven (player, GB), Antonio Jimenez (Coach, Spain) and Björn Hedmann (medical doctor, Sweden). The new committee represented the views of the different organizational areas within the sport of wheelchair basketball.

A FOUR CLASS SYSTEM was developed. It had been previously published in 1976 as a five class system (STROHKENDL 1974 & 1978) and introduced to the ISMGF Medical Committee. In 1982, at their Annual Meeting in Stoke Mandeville, the wheelchair basketball delegates voted unanimously in favour of the inclusion of other disabilities in international competition and adopted the new four class/13 team point system. The ISMGF Technical, Medical and the Executive Committees voted unanimously against this significant change. The basketball proposal was brought forward to the Council of Nations by the Sub-Section and was adopted by a 15 to 7 vote, two-thirds majority.

IN 1983 THE 3RD GOLD CUP was held in Halifax, Nova Scotia, Canada. Players with other disabilities were allowed to play for the first time in an ISMGF competition, but still under the old classification system. This major tournament was used to inform and to classify all existing players in readiness for the new system's implementation at the 1984 Paralympics. Stan Labanowich challenged the authority of the Medical Committee and subsequently the Executive Committee of the ISMGF by rejecting their insistence to remain involved in the classification process. As a result of this very necessary action by the Chairman of the Sub-Section for Wheelchair Basketball, the ISMGF Medical Committee and in particular its, Chairman, Cairbre McCann, adopted a defensive attitude. They resisted change and ultimately acted against the best interests of the players.

Canada's team at 3rd Gold Cup in Tampa, Florida 1979

1st time amputees are allowed to play at ISMGF sanctioned event in Halifax, Canada, 4th Gold Cup. Players: Murray Brown (l.) Roy Sherman, Canada

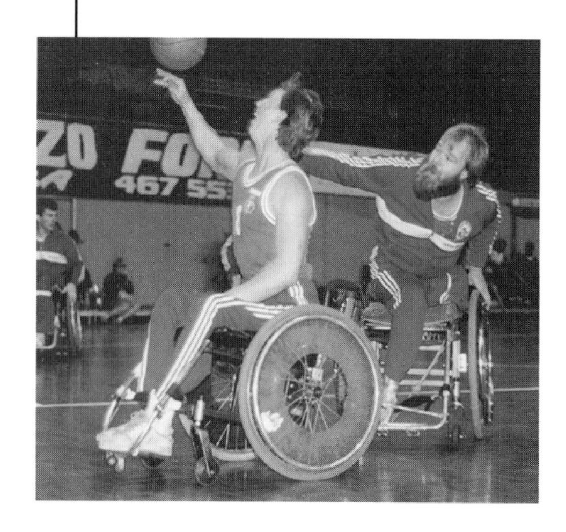

IN 1984, THE 6TH PARALYMPICS were held in Sto Mandeville after the US failed to organize this eve in Champaign/Urbana, Illinois. International whe chair basketball lost an opportunity to compete the area where its origins are rooted. Players wi disabilities other than spinal paralysis played f the first time in Stoke Mandeville in a Paralymp event. Wheelchair Basketball elected its new Ex cutive Committee consisting of Phil Craven, Reuv Heller, Don Perriman (Australia), Horst Strohken and Rob Verheuvel (The Netherlands), with St Labanowich as Chairman. Phil Craven became t first athlete to serve on an ISMGF Sport Section Ex cutive Committee and chaired the Player Classific tion Committee after the resignation of Horst Stro kendl from this position. The irony of this develo ment was that in1977, Philip Craven, was one of t individuals from the G.B. national team who w banned by Sir Ludwig Guttmann after a dispu concerning the suitability of coaches.

THE BITTER IRONY associated with thie conflict su rounding classification was that both parties tri to serve wheelchair sports to their best knowled and interest. The conflict came about because two very different views of persons with disabilitie On the one hand, there was the patronizing attitu of the medical doctors and their staff, whose pe ception was dominated by focusing on the disabi ty; on the other hand, there was the resolve towar self-determination by the players. This conflict w a painful one, particularly when the doctors we informed that experienced players were better qu lified than anyone else in classifying wheelcha basketball players (STROHKENDL 1985). The cla sification system for wheelchair basketball becan a means of self-determination. This phraseolo was expressed for the first time amongst the inte national authorities on the occasion of the Fir ISMGF Symposium, held on the 27th July 1985 Stoke Mandeville, but was understood by only few. Why then did Cairbre McCann and some of h colleagues still want to apply a medically base

Don Periman, Australia

classification system, one which was inferior in its results? The sole reason was that they could not see that they were dealing with highly trained and determined athletes who wished to govern the sport that they themselves invented. Their perception continued to be one of a doctor/patient relationship.

Philip Craven, GB, first player on the Executive Committee Wheelchair Basketball Section of the ISMGF in 1984: successor of Horst Strohkendl as Chairman of the Classification Committee

FINALLY, IN 1986, ISMGF gave up its reluctance to allow other disabilities at the Annual Games. In 1987, responsibility for classification passed in its entirety to the Wheelchair Basketball Section. The Medical Committee was told by the Basketball Section to stop imposing unnecessary medical examinations on the players, after the US team had refused for a second time to follow this procedure. Philip Craven, as Chairman of the Player Classification Committee, did not accept any compromise and always had the right arguments on his side. He possessed twenty years of experience as a player and had been the subject of a concept of rehabilitation which kept persons with disabilities in an underprivileged position. He rejected the stereotype of the *eternal patient* because it hindered the process of independence and self-determination. Unfortunately, the important contribution that could be made by experienced athletes in rehabilitation is still not properly understood by physicians and medical personnel in many parts of the world.

STAN LABANOWICH, a non-disabled person, has contributed immensely to the development and growth of wheelchair basketball. He had prepared the stage for Philip Craven and other persons with disabilities. He was predisposed to accept, as a consequence of his own and of Nugent's philosopy, that the important task of self-determination in wheelchair basketball and in rehabilitation could only be realized by the athletes themselves. Consequently, Philip Craven was elected Chairman of the ISMGF Wheelchair Basketball Section in 1988, on the occasion of the 8th Paralympiad in Seoul, Korea.

THE PROCESS OF CONSOLIDATION AND INDEPENDENCE AFTER 1988

THE EXECUTIVE COMMITTEE elected in Seoul provided a good mixture of old and new members. From the athlete's side, Phil Craven became the new Chairman. He was assisted by Armand „Tip" Thiboutot of the USA as Secretary, who was also a First Vice-President of his national basketball association (NWBA) as well as a former player and coach. The other members were Stan Labanowich (Competitions), Bernard Courbariaux (Classification), Horst Strohkendl (Officiating), Reuven Heller (Rules) and Tony Sainsbury (Development). The allocation of specific jobs and the demand for regular reports from the relevant subcommittees was designed to improve the accountability and the work output of the Basketball Section.

PHILIP CRAVEN REALISED quickly, that the name „Sub-Section of the ISMGF" was totally unsuitable for image and marketing purposes. In 1989, the name of International Wheelchair Basketball Federation (IWBF) was adopted and accepted by the International Stoke Mandeville Games Federation (ISMGF). That year, the Constitution was also modified to a form more akin to that of the FIBA model. The various IWBF subcommittees were changed into commissions and the Chairmen became Presidents. The subcommittees of Officiating and Rules were combined into the Technical Commission. This new approach signified the increased responsibility and independence of the commissions. The member nations of international wheelchair basketball were allocated to zones similar to FIBA. The Basketball Commission for the Disabled of FIBA established closer links to the IWBF through its President Jan Berteling of the Netherlands and its Vice-President Terry Barnett of England.

In response to the demand for the development and growth of wheelchair basketball which had been expressed at the Arnhem meeting in 1980, a closer relationship of the national wheelchair basketball organizations with the member organizations of FIBA was recommended. One of Stan Labanowich's greatest wishes was the affiliation of international wheelchair basketball with FIBA, with wheelchair basketball becoming part of the official FIBA programme. Even if this wish were to produce some benefits, the administrators of wheelchair basketball realized that their sport was still not sufficiently organized on a national level and was rarely affiliated with the national running basketball organisations of FIBA to justify such a union. The FIBA Commission for Basketball for the Disabled had one mandate: to assist all the disabled, not only persons in wheelchairs, to play basketball. The IWBF could only become a member of FIBA through a majority vote of the member countries of FIBA, the legislative body. The IWBF did not possess sufficient strength to be accepted and respected by FIBA as an equal partner in negotiations. The IWBF was not actually an independent Federation; it had no separate membership, no financial resources and had to rely on a few devoted volunteers. In 1989, the IWBF chose to concentrate on its internal development: Classification was consolidated following the last battle with ISMGF in 1987 and was now well administered by Bernard Courbariaux of France, who has chaired the classification commission since 1988 to date (1996).

Armand „Tip" Thiboutot, USA, second player to serve international wheelchair basketball as Secretary and Vice President, since 1992 as President Technical Commission IWBF

Executive Committee Wheelchair Basketball of the ISMGF in Stoke Mandeville 1989 (from left) Armand „Tip" Thiboutot, Tony Sainsbury (GB), Stan Labanowich (USA), Philip Craven (GB), Reuven Heller (Israel), Bernard Courbariaux (France), Horst Strohkendl (Germany)

The technical side of the game became more significant within the IWBF. Horst Strohkendl was President of the Technical Commission during one term from 1988 - 1992. He encouraged the IWBF to follow the FIBA rules and regulations where relevant, but not to adopt rules that were contrary to the spirit of the wheelchair game. Among other documents, a training curriculum for referees was developed (STROHKENDL & OTTO 1988). The basic rule interpretations as well as a complete rule book for wheelchair basketball were prepared. In 1992 „Tip" Thiboutot, a wheelchair basketball player and strong advocate of self-determination for players was elected President of the Technical Commission. He emphasized even greater player involvement. His contribution has helped guarantee the recognition of wheelchair basketball as a player-oriented, independent sport.

Development has become a major concern during the early 1990s. The recruitment of new nations to the federation assumed an importance equal to helping nations recruit new players for all levels of competition. Grass roots development was viewed as essential to the growth of the sport. Well-established wheelchair basketball programmes in member countries and good relations with all institutions that deal with sports for persons with disabilities represent the fundamental base of the Federation. However, because too few potential players take up wheelchair basketball, the urgent need for grassroots development is emphasized within the IWBF (see LYKINS 1991). Effective development and training will result in more players, more teams, better national teams and more attractive international tournaments. Reg McClellan of Canada, a national player for his country and Technical Director of the Canadian Wheelchair Basketball Association (CWBA) has been in charge of development since 1989. He strongly promoted the development of zones. In 1996 the work for international wheelchair basketball has become more decentralized. Thus far, the following zones have been established: European, Mediterranean, South American, Nortth American and Asian.

Whilst the IWBF remained part of the ISMWSF, only £ 600 sterling per annum was available to run the sport. The IWBF had no choice but to break away from its mother organization if it was to become financially viable. Some member countries of the ISMWSF refused to accept the independence of the IWBF because they concluded that greater membership fees would be charged not only by the IWBF, but b

Jan Bertling, FIBA Commission for Basketball for Persons with a Disabi

ll other sports as well. Philip Craven and his Com-ıittee members knew that it was impossible to rganize wheelchair basketball on the international ›vel without an increase in financial resources.

HE IWBF BECAME independent at the annual meeting eld in conjunction with the European Champion-hips in Berlin in 1993. Wheelchair basketball na-ons all over the world appreciate the work of the WBF and pay their annual fee because they realize ıat it benefits the sport. It is hoped that the IWBF vill consolidate its organization through the crea-on of a full-time Secre-ariat. No sport can ac-ually achieve anything n the international ›vel without the assis-ance of a well-functio-ing administration. We must realize and accept he fact that the essential funds will only be raised f the sport is well organized and succeeds in gai-ing public recognition. To achieve this lofty goal, he President, Philip Craven, had to assume the osition of Chief Executive Officer for a limited eriod of time.

INTERNATIONAL WHEELCHAIR basketball has always had to rely primarily on devoted individuals. The way to independence and self-determination always had and still has many obstacles. These are not only financial ones, as the history of the last 50 years has demonstrated. The IWBF will always include devoted individuals, who will contribute to the success of wheelchair basketball as a wonderful sport and who try to bring meaning to their lives. To paraphrase Nugent's thesis again: a disability is not necessarily a disaster but a challenge of life which may strengthen character, that part of the players' psyche which cannot generally be classified as disabled. This strong belief can even help to transcend the experience of wheelchair basketball to experience real human values and achieve a better understanding between all members of our respective societies.

Ricardo Moreno, Spain, President Competition Commission IWBF since 1992, int. Referee

Horst Strohkendl, Chairman (since 1990 President) of the Technical Commission IWBF

Bernard Courbariaux, successor of Philip Craven as Chairman (since 1990 President) of the Classification Commission in 1988

Development Committee IWBF (from left, front) Escort, Reg McClellan, Katsuyuki Hamamoto (JPN), (back) Escort, Menzo Barrisch (RSA), Rizk Mazri (Jordan), Sheila Bastos (Brazil), Bob Szyman (USA), Escort, Tony Sainsbury (GB)

Reg McClellan, Canada, President Development Commission IWBF since 1990

Kathleen Curtis, USA, Educational Resources Co-ordinator, int. Classifier

THE HISTORY OF WOMEN'S WHEELCHAIR BASKETBALL

Who was the first woman to play wheelchair basketball or even netball? The photo shows...

...ONE OF THE FIRST COURAGEOUS WOMEN WHO PLAYED WHEELCHAIR BASKETBALL ON A MEN'S TEAM. REHABILITATION MAY NOT HAVE PLAYED A PROMINENT ROLE IN ENCOURAGING THE FIRST WOMEN TO PLAY.

THEIR INITIAL participation can probably be attributed to a natural desire to compete and to enjoy the game, to challenge the men. We assume that these were, and remain the primary motives for women who wish to play competitive wheelchair basketball.

TEAMS COMPOSED OF WOMEN are not prevalent in wheelchair basketball. Even in countries with a long tradition of involvement in wheelchair basketball, only 10% of all players are females and these countries rarely organize competition in leagues and national championships. The reasons for these deficits are quite obvious: fewer women play sports and fewer women are disabled in comparision to men. Only twenty percent of all paraplegics are women. In many countries, basketball programmes are not promoted for women; for a long time that was even true of the USA. Women who have played wheelchair basketball perhaps even more than men, have been forced to respond to the typically biased question: *Are the baskets as high as in the regular game?* The psychological barriers that they had to overcome should not be underestimated.

1st woman playing at Stoke Mandeville in 1949

ON THE OTHER HAND, female wheelchair basketball players have contributed greatly to changing the attitudes towards women with disabilities in society. The challenge for women to accept their disability and to adapt to a new identity can be expected to be even greater than it is for men. Women play wheelchair basketball beautifully, one more reason to promote this sport for this very important minority.

THE FOUNDING OF *Les Wheelchair Wonderettes* from Quebec, probably the first female team in the world, was connected to an exceptionally devoted and charismatic person, namely, BILL HEPBURN, one of Canada's most proficient originators of wheelchair sports. In 1951, he gathered paraplegics in the Montreal area and founded the *Wheelchair Wonders*, the first wheelchair sports club in Canada. I assume that he wondered how men and women can compensate and achieve success in life, regardless of their severe physical disabilities. Bill Hepburn must have experienced deep satisfaction, when he succeeded in sending the first men's team from North America to Stoke Mandeville in 1953, only the second International Games (AQSFR 1993).

THE APPEARANCE of Les Wonderettes at Quebec in 1957 represents a true miracle in the evolution of wheelchair basketball. Because of his many successful initiatives in Canada, Hepburn deserves to be inducted into the Basketball Hall of Fame in Springfield, Massachusetts. Bill Hepburn certain would agree with the statement: *The history sports for the disabled is the history of devote persons who succeeded in overcoming all th great difficulties and especially the many unex pected limitations caused by ignorant an anxious fellow citizens. – Quelle richesse de vo souvenirs et de la qualité de votre experienc Merci beaucoup Bill Hepburn!*

A MAJOR INITIATIVE in the development of wheelcha basketball for women was taken by Israel on th occasion of the 3rd Paralympiad in Tel Aviv in 196

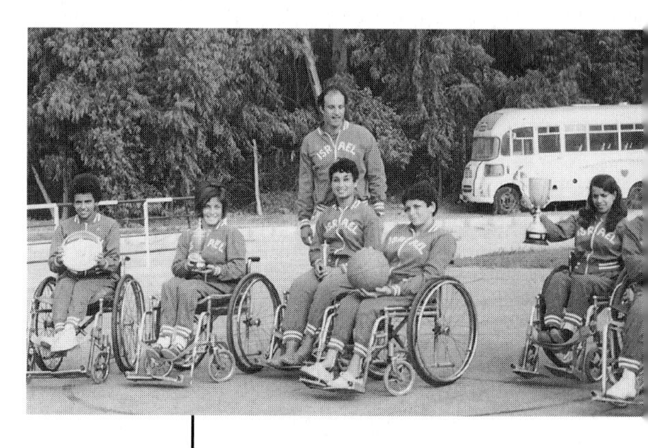

Israel's women team: winner of the 1st Paralympic Tournament in Tel Av on the occasion of th 3rd Paralympia in Israel 1968. 3rd from left: Zippora Rosenberg-Rubin

(HUBERMAN 1968). Israel organized the fir international competition for national teams com posed of women. Five countries entered a team Argentina, Austria, Great Britain, Israel and th USA. With the exception of Israel and Argentin who offered well-established basketball progran mes for the many individuals with polio in thei countries, the teams were selected from athlete who competed primarily in other sports.

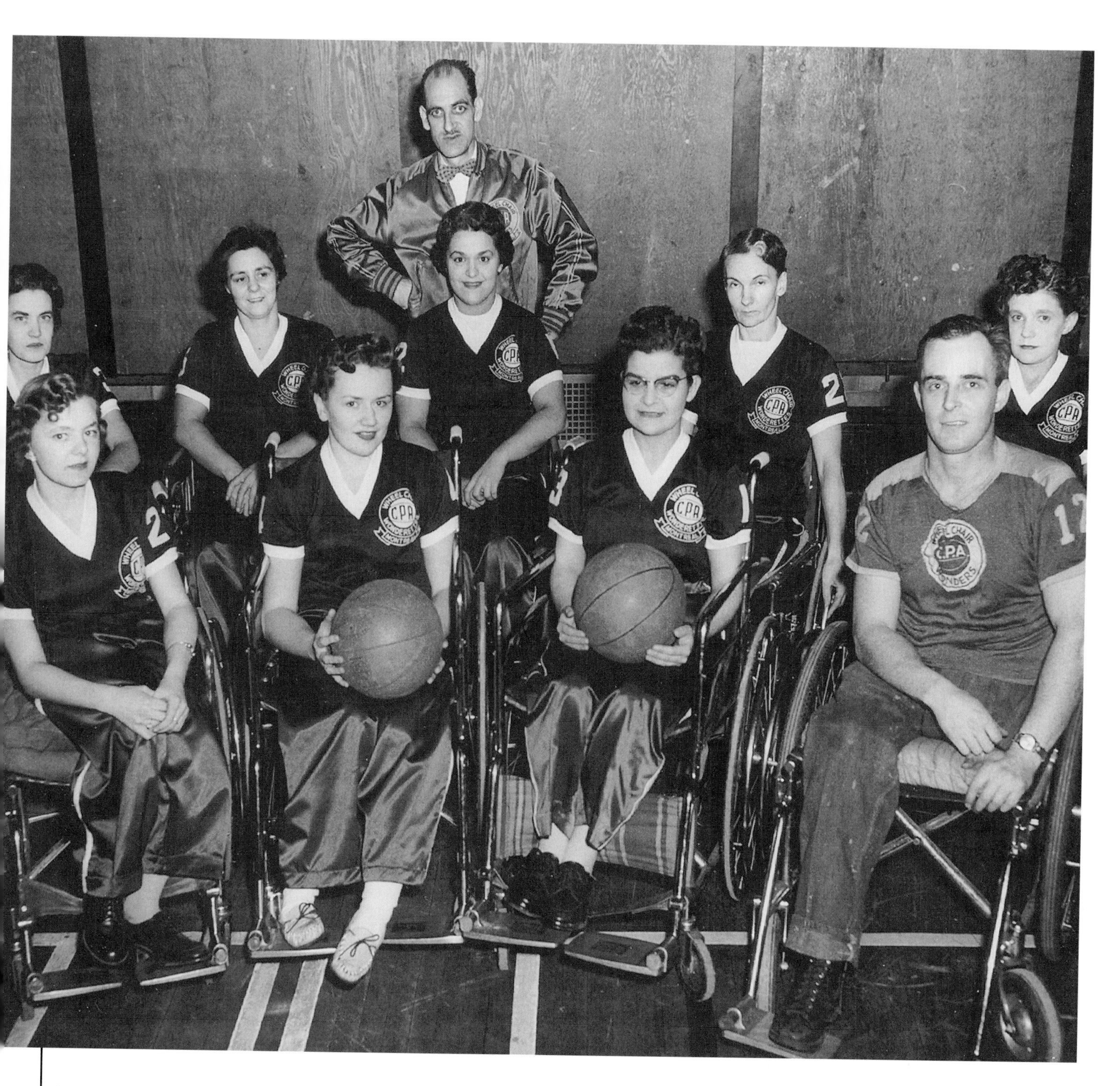

Les Wheelchair Wonderetts 1957. 1st women's team from Quebec: in front from left: Jeanie Parks, Clymar Sowery, Janet Anderson and Jean Paul Rochon (ass. coach); second row: Thérèse Tourangeau, Thérèse Drolet, Gisèle Lamoureux, Bertha Gilbert, Isabelle Harris and the founder Bill Hepburn

USA's women team 1968 –
3rd Paralympiad Tel Aviv, Israel 1968

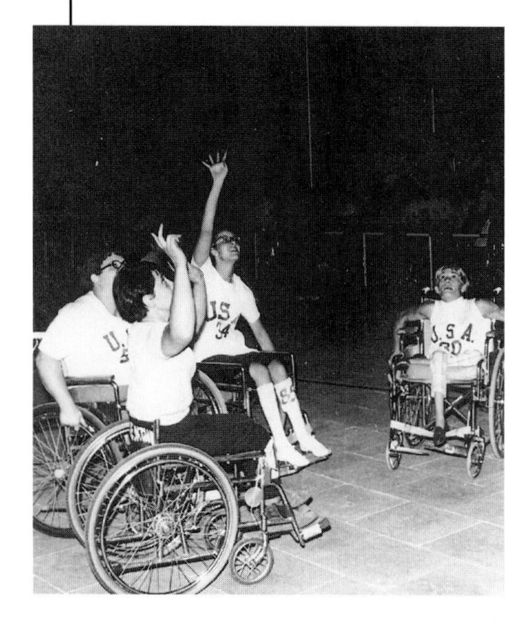

THE RULES CONTAINED two significant modifications compared with those for men:

- The ball was a mini-basketball (lighter and smaller).
- The free-throw line was drawn 1 m in advance of the conventional line.

THE LEVEL OF COMPETITION must have been very low compared with the present day level of play. Israel's young team captured the gold medal, defeating Argentina 17 to 12. USA won the bronze medal by defeating Austria 10 to 7 in another low-scoring game compared to current performances, where the best teams often score 40 or more points. Zipporah Rosenberg Rubin of Israel started her long international career as a basketball player.

IN 1970, THE FIRST women's tournament took place in Stoke Mandeville, where Argentina was placed first, Great Britain second and Jamaica third. We

Hector Ramirez: Promoter of wheelchair basketball in Argentina

wonder who was the motivating force behind the team from Jamaica? Having consulted Joan Scruton, one of the three musceteers of the Stoke Mandeville Games, on this question Ralf Hill-Jones from England was identified as the person who helped to develop wheelchair basketball in Jamaica. Hector Ramirez, a Stoke Mandeville enthusiast, was obviously the driving force in Argentina. On one occasion, he even travelled by ship with his team to England.

IN 1972, 7 TEAMS entered the 4th Paralympiad in Heidelberg, Germany. Israel, Argentina, Great Britain and Jamaica were the most internationally experienced teams. Canada sent a novice team, the successors of les Wheelchair Wonderettes. Germany and Yugoslavia, both novice teams, completed the field. The favourites, Israel, were unexpectedly beaten by a surprisingly strong team from Jamaica in the semi-final. Argentina qualified for the final by defeating Germany. Argentina then succeeded in capturing the Gold Medal with a victory over Jamaica, 28 to 25. Israel punished the inexperienced German team 37 to 5, thereby exacting some compensation for their earlier defeat at the hands of Jamaica.

DURING AN UNOFFICIAL MEETING of the wheelchair ba ketball representatives of the attending nations, th manager of the Canadian women's team, Donal Royer, strongly recommended applying the sam rules for women and men. The representativ from Europe did not support this recommendatic based on the assumption that it would further di courage women from playing wheelchair baske ball. Royer's sports-oriented attitude proved victo rious; it found greater acceptance than a few pess mists had expected. Women wheelchair basketba players began training more seriously and regula ly. Wheelchair basketball for women surpassed th level of rehabilitation and recreation. It evolve into a true sport.

THE SMALL NUMBER OF TEAMS competing at the intern tional level hindered the progress of wheelcha basketball for women. Teams from Austria an Yugoslavia competed only once. Jamaica's tea disappeared after 1976. France started with a goo team in 1973, winning the tournament at Stok Mandeville. Unfortunately, France disappeared fo 7 years following 1974 after it had lost in the fin match of the first European Championship in Ke pape, France to an unexpectedly strong Germa team by the score of 35 to 20. A team from the US did not compete in 1972 in Heidelberg. The femal players who competed in 1976 in Toronto at th Paralympic Games were not the best players ava lable.

THE WEAKEST POINT IN women's wheelchair basketba is the very small or even non-existent base of pla yers available at the national level. Intensified wor at the grass roots level is essential to improv women's wheelchair basketball. Countries deceiv themselves if they believe that by forming women's team consisting of a minimum number players, they can initiate programmes throug competition at the international level. This kind effort is counter-productive and usually fails produce a broad base of players at home.

HE SITUATION IN GERMANY was not different from ther countries. The desperate need to publicize heelchair sports, especially for women athletes, as at first stronger than the need to establish a ell-organized national programme for women's

Israel's women team 1972, participants at the 4th Paralympiad 1972 in Heidelberg. 3rd Rachel Said, 4th Ariela Cohen-Mizan, 5th Zipporah Rosenberg-Rubin (from left)

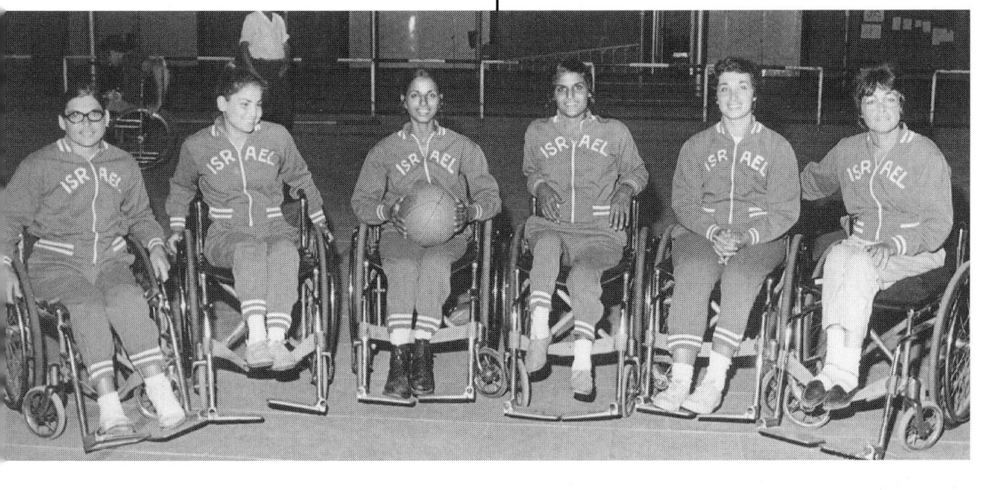

Bob Szyman, USA, promoter of women and junior programmes

asketball. Germany was, however, lucky to pos- ss, by chance, a few very talented players STROHKENDL 1994). Because of the old medical assification system, the German team was able to eld the best players in each class: Regina Isecke point), Rita Laux (2 points) and Rita Breuer (3 oints). *The German Fräulein Wonder* was born 1975, following their first defeat of the strong nd confident team from Israel by a score of 45 to 1 at Stoke Mandeville. The coach of this surpri- ngly strong team was Horst Strohkendl, who gai- ed some international recognition due to his am's success.

HE EVENTUAL DOMINANCE of the German team was elayed in 1976 in Toronto, Canada, at the Para- mpic tournament by a superbly coached team om Israel. The coach, Danny Shahar, imposed a ll-court press and used his stronger bench effec- vely to neutralize the superior outside shooting of e German team. Israel won 39 to 32. Germany issed Rita Breuer who did not play in Toronto. aying with her in future tournaments, Germany

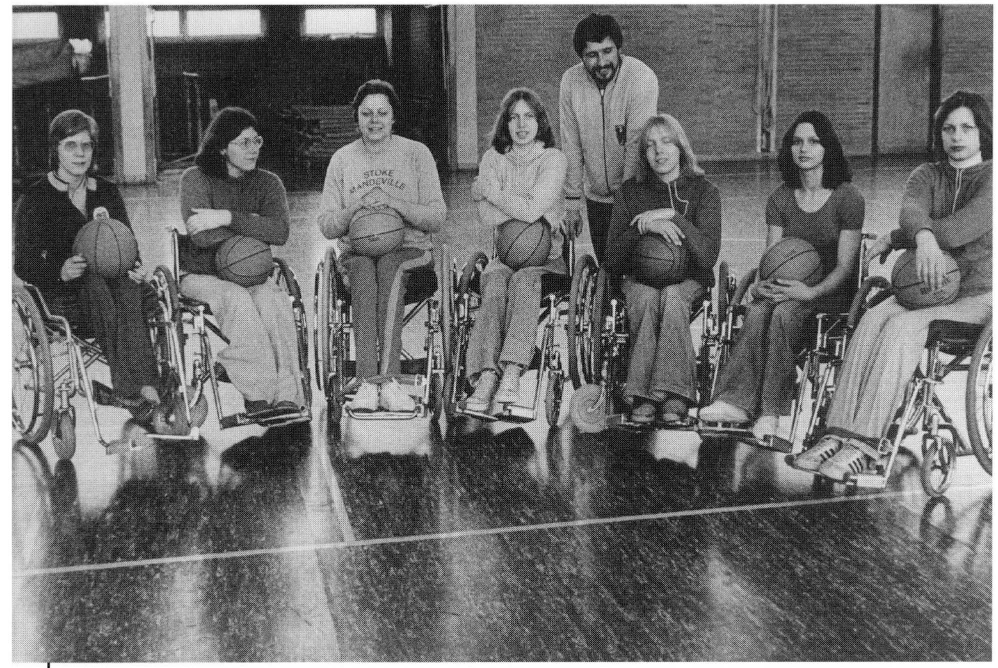

„German Fräulein Wonder" 1976: (from left) Gaby Hartwig, Martina Tschötschel, Rita Laux, Rita Breuer, Silke Boll, Gisela Hermes, Regina Isecke.
Coach: Horst Strohkendl (standing behind)

remained undefeated at all major tournaments untill 1988, when a strong USA team won the final at the 8th Paralympics in Seoul, Korea.

THE DOMINANCE of the German team and of the first runner-up from Israel in all major events after 1976 caused a decline in the number of women's teams. Only four teams participated at the 6th Paralympics in Arnhem in 1980. Germany won the Gold by outscoring Israel 58 to 37. The US team's improvement represented a positive development for the sport. Bob Szyman, a tireless supporter of wheelchair sports on all levels, was a major contributor a lot to the development of the national programme for wheelchair basketball in the USA (SZYMAN 1982). With Sharon Rahn taking leadership as well as Susan Hagel, both superb all-around athletes, the US team won the bronze medal by defeating Argentina 31 to 8.

Susan Hagel, USA: excellent all-round athlete and wheelcair basketball player

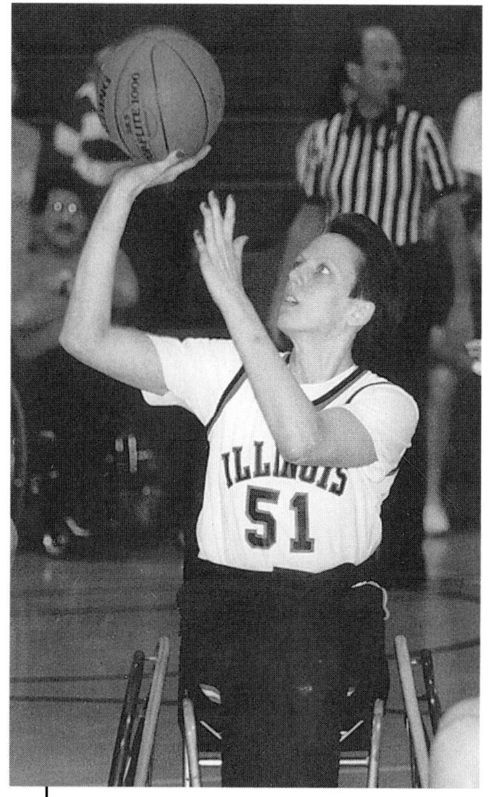

Sharon Rahn Hedrick, USA: excellent all-round athlete and wheelcair basketball player

FROM 1984 ONWARDS, women's wheelchair basketball gained more momentum. Japan entered a team coached by Shoko Kitamura for the first time at the Paralympic Games, staged at Stoke Mandeville in 1984. Wheelchair basketball for women was first played in Japan by the *Tokio Grace* in 1975 and then gradually developed. A US team was invited in 1981 to play in Japan and to assist the Japanese players in adjusting to the international level of *play* (SZYMAN 1982). Japan had come to Stoke Mandeville with a well-prepared team and demonstrated that Germany could be defeated, but it ultimately lost after holding a 10-point lead in th second half. Canada came back with the third gene ration of Les Wonderettes, among them a youn and talented player named Chantal Benoit. Th Netherlands fielded a team with strong 4-poi players, but had difficulties developing players i the 1 and 2-point categories. The failure of the US to organize the seventh Paralympic Games delaye their improvement for they did not win a medal a Stoke Mandeville. Germany and Israel dominate

Japan - USA 1981: USA's wheelchair basketball teams toured Japan

Japan's women team 1984: participated at the 7th Paralympiad in Stoke Mandeville, England 1984. Standing left: Shoko Kitamura

Deborah Sunderman, USA:
topscorer at 8th Paralympiad 1988
in Seoul, Korea

Heidi Kirste, Germany:
outstanding 1.5-player and top-scorer of the German team

for the last time by winning the Gold and Silver medal, as in the previous competitions. Japan won its first medal, the Bronze, by defeating the team from Canada.

The USA's well-developed national wheelchair basketball programme produced positive results in 1988 at Seoul, Korea (HEDRICK 1985; HEDRICK & HEDRICK 1991). Most of the USA players came from the two top women's teams: the university based *Illinois Fightin' Illini'* and *the Rolling Gophers* from Minnesota. Sharon Hedrick (formerly Rahn) was more than ably assisted by Deb Sunderman, who along with Brad Hedrick as Coach formed an excellent team. Germany succeeded in developing some new players, who provided hope of maintaining its supremacy in women's basketball. With Heidi Kirste (1.5 points) and Britt Tuna (1 point) they possessed the strongest players in these categories. The USA team proved stronger in the 4-point categories with Deb Sunderman, Sue Grimes and Barbara Yoss. The match was actually dominated by Deb Sunderman's superb outside shooting, as she scored 21 points. The USA ended the German team's long winning streak with a 38 to 31 victory. The bronze medal was won by the team from the Netherlands who defeated Canada 44 to 30.

Brad Hedrick, USA:
coach of USA's Gold Medal team
in Seoul, Korea 1988

Britt Tuna, Germany:
excellent 1-point player

Chantal Benoit Nr. 9: Canada's future,
guarded by Mary Ann O'Neil, USA No. 4

Successors of the „German Fräulein Wonder" 1988

In 1990, at the 1st World Wheelchair Basketball Championships in St. Etienne, France. Australia arrived with a young and talented team. But ultimately the superpowers USA and Germany met in the final, where Germany hoped to gain revenge for its defeat in Seoul. In one of the best matches ever played by women, the USA won the championship 58 to 55 despite Heidi Kirste's 23 points. Kirste's great individual performance proved insufficient against a well-balanced opponent. Canada, however, succeeded in exacting revenge for its defeat against the Netherlands in 1988 by winning its first medal in international competition.

Canada's women won their first Gold medal in 1992 at the 9th Paralympic Games in Barcelona, defeating the USA 35 to 25.Their victory came as a surprise since the teams from USA, Netherlands and even Germany were ranked higher based on their performance in preliminary matches. But Canada who had appointed in Tim Frick, an experienced and gifted coach, had undertaken long term plans with this goal in mind. The talented Chantal Benoit played the match of her life in the final by scoring 18 of her team's 35 points. The USA team could not replicate performances it had given earlier in the tournament. Credit must be given to Tim Frick for devising the stifling defence that limited the strong USA team to only 25 points. The Netherlands, who actually expected a better result, managed to capture only the Bronze Medal from a surprisingly strong Australian team. Germany however learned that previous success does not guarantee victory in sports and that defeat is an agonizing experience. The team's fifth place finish was the lowest since the team started playing internationally in 1972.

Canadian's women's team in 1992: Gold Medal winners in 1992, 9th Paralympiad in Barcelona, Spain

In 1994 at the second World Championships in Stoke Mandeville, Canada again proved to be the strongest team as they introduced a new star to the international scene, Renée Ledrew, a power forward who more than capably complemented guard Chantal Benoit's outside game. With the exception of Australia, which exchanged fourth place for third place with the Netherlands, the tournament results were identical to 1992 as the same teams captured the first five places.

Chantal Benoit, (No. 9) guarded by Mandy Rose (No. 7, Australia) at 2nd World Championships in Stoke Mandeville 1994

Tim Frick, Canada: coached the Canadian Gold Medal Team in Barcelona 1992 and at the 2nd World Championships in Stoke Mandeville 1994

: NEXT PARALYMPIC WHEELCHAIR BASKETBALL tourna-
nt in Atlanta will include eight female teams who
l undoubtedly demonstrate the best women's
eelchair basketball ever. Will the European
ms or Australia be strong enough to stop the
rth American dominance? The great Marja Lok-
: from the Netherlands is still pursuing her first
ralympic title. Lisel Tesch may even lead Austra-
to the top in anticipation of the major competi-
ns scheduled in Sydney for 1998 and 2000. Bra-

Renée Ledrew No. 8, Canada: power forward, at 2nd World Championships in Stoke Mandeville 1994

as a new team representing South and Central
erica, may not be strong enough to challenge
other more experienced teams. But Germany,
eat Britain and Japan are always good for an
expected result.

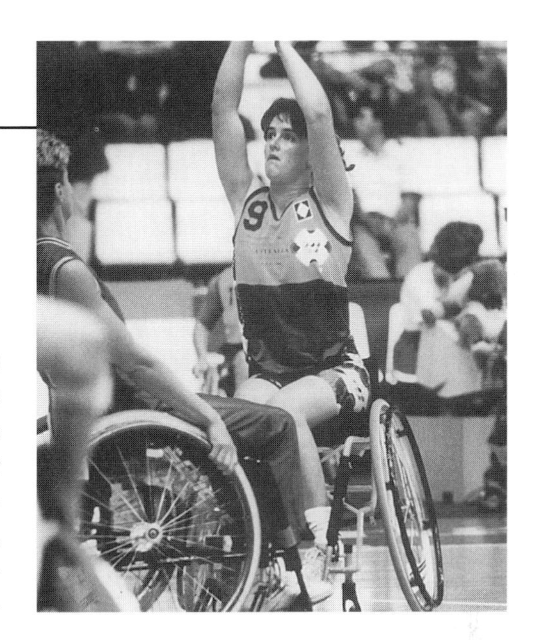

Liesl Tesch, Australia

THE QUALIFICATION TOURNAMENT for Atlanta has shown that the base for women's wheelchair basketball is still too small. Actually, only the following countries provide programmes for wheelchair basketball for women: Argentina, Australia, Brazil, Canada, France, Germany, Great Britain, Israel, Japan, Mexico, the Netherlands, Spain and the USA. On the threshold preparing to form teams are Sweden and Jordan. Will anyone reactivate the teams in Austria, Jamaica, Ireland and in the former Yugoslavia? Where are the devoted individuals who will promote wheelchair basketball for women in the future? The best ambassadors are the female players themselves. Do not hesitate to grasp reins and lead your country to a bright future.

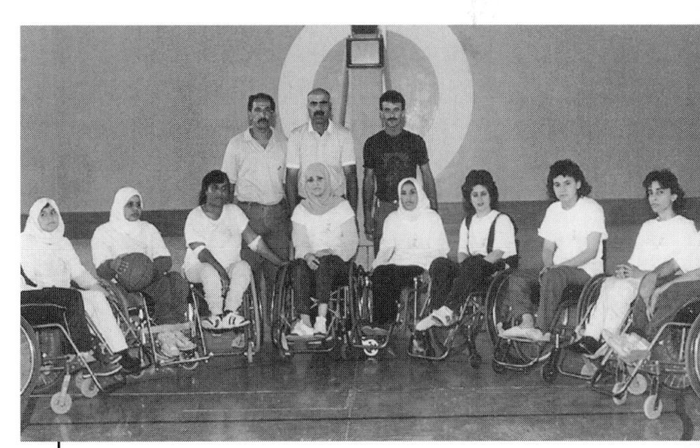

Women's wheelchair basketball in Amman, Jordan 1990. Standing second from left: Rizk Masri, promoter of wheelchair basketball in Jordan and the Mediteranean Zone

Israel - the Netherlands, Marja Lokker, 6th European Championships, Delden, the Netherlands 1995

Barcelona '92

OFFICIATING

THECHNIQUE

IN THE EARLY YEARS OF WHEELCHAIR BASKETBALL, IN THE MID AND LATE FORTIES, THE PLAYERS AND THE TEAMS IN THE UNITED STATES OF AMERICA (USA)...

...EXPERIMENTED A GREAT DEAL IN ORDER TO FIND APPROPRIATE RULES FOR THE GAME. RUNNING BASKETBALL SERVED AS A DISTANT MODEL.

THE PLAYERS PERCEIVED great differences, particularly as a result of using old and heavy wheelchairs. The team from Kansas City even allowed intentional charging and called themselves "Bulldozers". The early game resembled a mixture of basketball and football (LABANOWICH 1975, 34); but of great significance was the fact that the players resisted advice to lower the baskets.

Charly Attkinson, besides Sir Ludwi Guttmann and Joan Scruton one of three musketeers in Stoke Mandevi officiates wheelchair netball in 195 between the teams of Lyme Green Settlement and Pan American Jets (final score 7 - 14)

One of the first Officials, Galesburg, Illinois, in 1949:
1st NWBA Championship

THE GAME EVOLVED and more non-disabled persons joined wheelchair basketball as coaches, administrators and especially as referees. Having running basketball as a major resource of playing experience, many of these individuals were encouraged to apply forcefully a policy, which would design the rules of the wheelchair game to adhere as closely as possible to the original version of basketball. This concept of assimilation with running basketball is still followed in most of our member countries. The technical people had focused primarily on the written rules of running basketball and experienced great difficulties in formulating adequate rules to define dribbling and progressing with the ball.

THE CONSTITUTIONAL mother organization of the IWBF, the NWBA of the USA, guaranteed strong influence and input from the players on all issues involving wheelchair basketball from the first day of its foundation in 1949 (read the concept of self-determination at pp. 20). Therefore, it was no surprise that the players created very simple and appropriate *dribbling and progressing with the ball* rules for wheelchair basketball. On the other hand, the technical officials appointed at Stoke Mandeville since 1958, primarily referees from the running game, tortured their brains, as well as the players, in order to define *the dribbling and the progressing with the ball* rules. They proposed a complicat mixture of pushing, steering, pivoting and dribbli which they wanted to correspond as closely as po sible to the written rules of FIBA. Fortunately, inte national wheelchair basketball adopted the liber lized rules of the NWBA in 1973 when Stan Lab nowich of the USA and Reuven Heller of Isra strongly promoted these rules at the first meeting the newly established Sub-Section for Wheelcha Basketball of the ISMGF.

In the late seventies, representatives of international wheelchair basketball perceived important differences between wheelchair basketball and running basketball. The USA, once the leader in developing rules governing the wheelchair game, appears to have abdicated its former role in the formulation of wheelchair specific rules and guidelines defining not only how the game should be played, but also in relation how referees should be trained. Perhaps they have become reluctant to distance themselves from the official rules of the NCAA and the NBA, and as a consequence, from the evolving and highly admired models of running basketball? The coaching side of the game developed very well, which is evident in several publications on coaching (see SHAVER 1981, OWEN 1982 and HEDRICK et al. 1994). A more reasonable explanation for this bias in the development of these two important segments of the game in the NWBA is the fact that officiating is not a principle interest of the players.

Official at 2nd Paralympiad in Tokyo 1964

Three major issues began to influence the development of the wheelchair basketball rules:

- 1. Investigations on the essential reasons for, and the process of, rule changes in FIBA.
- 2. The specific movements of a wheelchair in basketball (versus moving on legs).
- 3. International policy, which invites all individuals with physical disabilities to experience wheelchair basketball.

Present influences and objectives in the IWBF

FIBA and other recognized basketball federations define the objectives of the game of basketball. Of great importance are criteria which help in defining the ideal of this unique team game. FIBA's Technical Committee always endeavours, through its members, to continually improve the rules and thereby safeguard basketball's fundamental qualities and ultimately realize its perceived ideal.

Continuous dribbling in wheelchair basketball, 6th European Championships, Delden, the Netherlands 1995

The major objectives and criteria of the game of basketball could read as follows:

- *Athletic demands and skillfulness,*
- *No intentional physical contact, Variable team play, including all players,*
- *Balance of offensive and defensive actions supporting the game's fluency and its unpredictability,*
- *Highly demanding mental challenge associated with the combination of precision under stress and control of behaviour*

The above criteria are not comprehensive. The written rules constitute a very fine balance between the offensive and the defensive actions of the players. The various rule committees in basketball refer to the above criteria in addressing emerging discrepancies in the actual conduct of the game. The players' desire for excellence may influence this balance as well. For example, very successful long-range shooting reduces the element of uncertainty brought about by good defence and also reduces the amount of exciting play in the area near the basket.

The commercialization of the sport of basketball has introduced other influences (for example: more physical contact is tolerated in order to provide a stimulating spectacle for the spectators or to satisfy the interests of the mass-media and the sponsors) which have exerted a significant impact on the rules and the conduct of the game. Many of these rules are not necessarily applicable for IWBF competitions. The IWBF still regards wheelchair basketball within the framework of an amateur sport ethic.

German collaborators on wheelchair officiating since 1979: Werner Otto (left) and Horst Strohkendl

THE EVOLUTION OF wheelchair basketball which was developed by the players and to a lesser extent by the coaches, reveals the impending structure and the essential conditions concerning the game. This development cannot be naturally perceived by the officials without special training. Referees tend to follow patterns learned from running basketball.

AN INITIAL ANALYSIS of the movement of a wheelchair and the skills required to control this movement was published in 1981 (see STROHKENDL, RAES 1982). It was refined in 1988 by STROHKENDL/ OTTO and by the Technical Commission of the IWBF in 1991. Compared with the running, pivoting, jumping and stopping of running basketball players, the specific basketball repertoire in a wheelchair is more limited and essentially different: Braking, stopping, steering, turning on the spot, moving to the side, crossing the path of another wheelchair, moving backwards, all frequently executed while handling the ball, are not only much different in appearance and execution in a wheelchair when compared to a player using his legs; but they also have a significant impact on **the balance of offensive and defensive actions,** which is defined and controlled by the rules. If we agree that the fundamental principles and criteria of basketball are the same for FIBA and the IWBF, the written rules of wheelchair basketball must be, to some extent, described differently in order to serve the very nature of the wheelchair game.

DRIBBLING AND PROGRESSING with the ball are defir more simply (compare Art. 38 and 39, IWBF R Book 1995); but even then the player with the b still realizes his disadvantage in „1 against 1" p compared with running basketball. The necessity manoeuvre a wheelchair and to control the b with the hands at the same time, significantly lin the offensive opportunities of a wheelchair bask ball player. However, screening with a wheelch has become the most effective skill in obtain favourable positions on court or in providing a m match and consequently good scoring opportu ties. These two very specific elements of wheelch basketball favour the development of team stra gies which emphasize execution away from the b They create mismatches over the entire distance the court, for example: screening in the backco by an offensive player(s); pick and roll on the we side in the halfcourt. Screening in the backcourt not an effective tac in running basketb due to the fact t players can „slid through screens deny a mismatch, o two on one advanta (TECHNICAL CO MISSION; IWBF 199

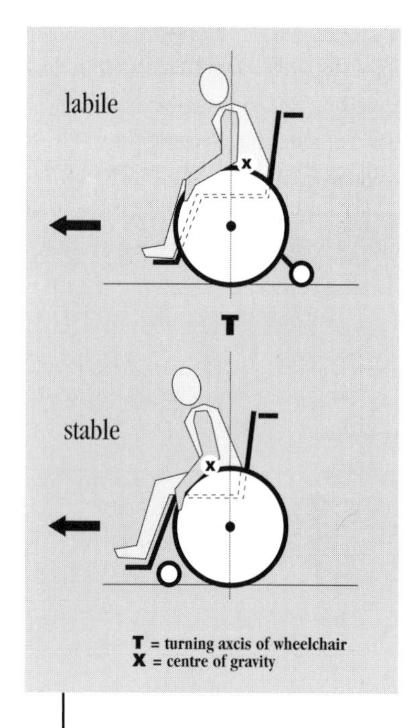

Difference in forward rolling stability

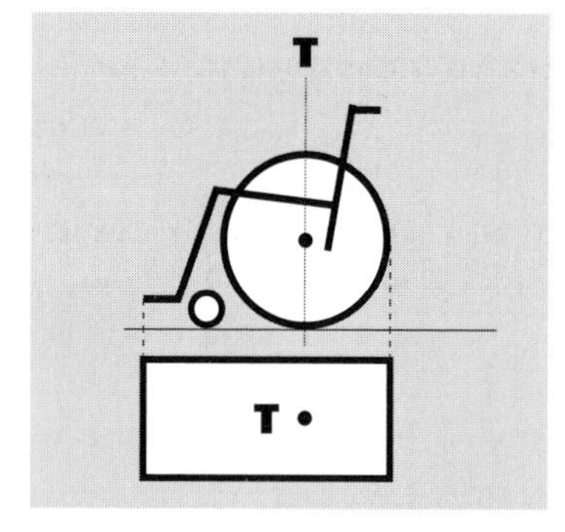

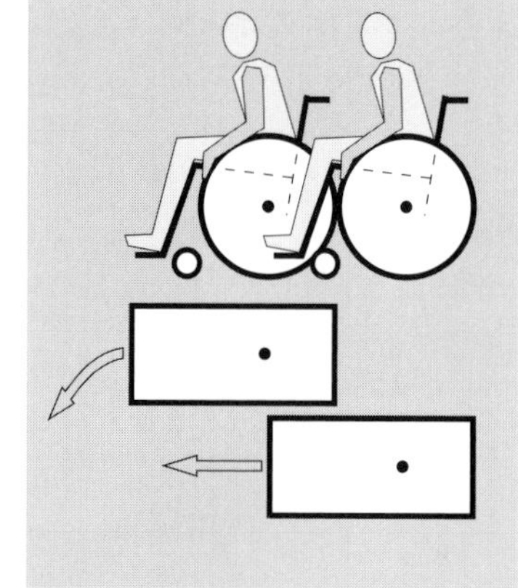

Crossing the path correctly: Axle of the backwheel is front of the most protruding part of the opponent's wheelchair

1st IWBF clinic on officiating in conjunction with FIBA, Treviso, Italy May 1990. From left: Luc Raes, Belgium (IWBF treasurer since 1992), Itzhack Ramot, Israel and Bob Beacock, GB

RT. 47, *the Personal Foul*, in wheelchair basket-all and in its related interpretations, precisely efines the significant differences that exist bet-een it and the running version of the game. eeping in mind that in wheelchair basketball, the efence gains greater advantage in attacking the layer with the ball, screening in wheelchair bas-etball therefore favours the offensive player. „Posi-on“ becomes the crucial difference when compa-ing picking and screening between running and heelchair basketball. In running basketball, the layer has established a legal position if he stands pright with both feet on court. Most decisions on uls are related to this image. In wheelchair bas-etball, this concept is obviously not applicable. he direction and speed of the moving wheelchair, hange of direction and the distance of the two noving opponents (the ball can be involved) are ne main points of reference defining fouls, as well s accidental contact or negligible contact in heelchair basketball. The official must sense the ntent of the player who normally focuses on occu-ying a favourable free position for his team on ourt.

VEN A LAYMAN understands that a wheelchair basket-all player cannot stop immediately on the spot and nust turn his wheelchair before moving to a lateral osition on court; typical lateral sliding is not pos-ible in a wheelchair. In order to understand cor-ect braking, steering and crossing the path of an pponent's wheelchair, as well as all the opportu-ities that exist to hold an opponent's wheelchair, onsiderable experience and acute observation kills are required. Screening, involving primarily wo or more players, has such a great impact on the ntire game of wheelchair basketball, that team trategies (ex. backpicking) are significantly different from running basketball. That is the main reason why the IWBF has developed its own officiating technique on positioning and on co-operation between referees.

THE IWBF BELIEVES THE NECESSITY of a player classification system, thus providing real playing opportunities at all levels of competition for persons with varied physical disabilities (CLASSIFICATION COMMISSION, IWBF 1996). The rationale for this policy contains among others, the following main arguments:

- Wheelchair basketball was developed for those individuals who can not walk or run, but must use a wheelchair. For most paraplegics, wheelchair basketball is the only team game providing an opportunity to reach the international level.

- Wheelchair basketball is an amateur sport, which benefits the players first. The spectators are second. The desire for elite performance is accompanied by the obligation to include as many players as possible in the sport of wheelchair basketball. Two major guidelines are provided to serve this purpose: First, to organize increased playing opportunities on the national as well as on the international levels, taking into account a potential population that is mostly heterogeneous with regard to the nature of disability and residual physical potential; the second guideline involves the application of a proper classification system that motivates the teams to include players with more severe disabilities.

■ The IWBF regards development at grass-roots level as a major objective of its constitution and actual policy. This task is very difficult to fulfil and in essence very different from conventional sport. The representatives of wheelchair basketball organizations should make themselves aware of the instances of newly injured or congenitally impaired individuals, some lying in hospitals or sitting isolated at home, others living in institutions, waiting for suitable assistance and an opportunity to participate.

■ Recruiting new players means much more than serving the growth of wheelchair basketball and providing for the natural replacement of aging players by younger ones. Recruitment of new players from institutions complements most effectively their rehabilitation and requires specialized knowledge as well as complete commitment from the persons in charge (LYKINS 1991). Classification can prevent individuals with severe disabilities from dropping out when they start to compete in organized programmes.

■ The philosphy of self-determination for persons with disabilities presumes that they can master their limitations and learn to accept a new identity. Through a well-applied classification system, players with severe disabilities can reach the highest level of competition. Wheelchair basketball is represented by different types of players who become ambassadors for all their potential peers. The novice finds the type of player with whom he can identify (STROHKENDL 1991).

■ The acceptance of the classification system is based on the belief in fairness and on the solidarity of all players, solidarity not only with more physically impaired players of comparable level of proficiency, but also with the new and inexperienced ones. The latter are involved in the process of learning about and overcoming their disability. In fact, no better form of help for a novice exists than the assistance of an experienced and confident player. Unfortunately, this expertise is still rarely used in rehabilitation.

To summarize, the following diagram outlines the structure of the different entities that influence the rules of wheelchair basketball:

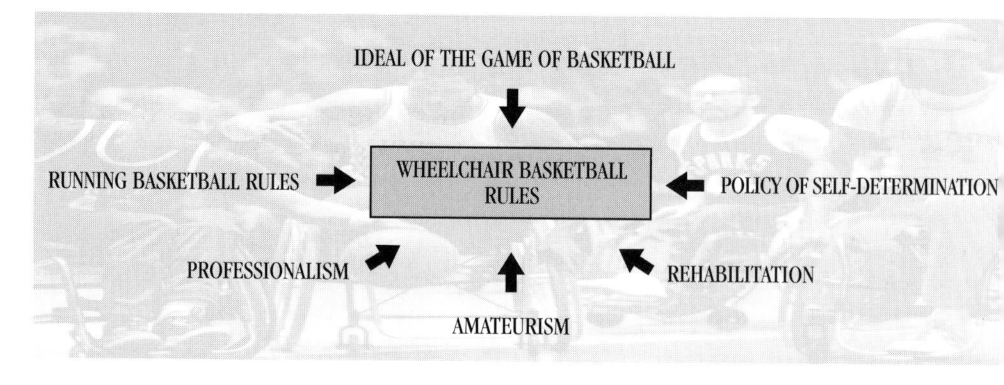

This recognition of the special objectives of the IWBF should not prevent the development of wheelchair basketball as an elite sport. There is no better means to promote self-determination among persons with disabilities throughout society than to organize wheelchair basketball as a true, attractive and elite sport. Proper development of rules and regulations, as well as a wheelchair basketball specific officiating technique, will serve elite performance.

An equitable classification system reflects the special objectives of the IWBF with regard to its unique population. Officiating must adhere to the fundamental principle of basketball as a non-contact game. The more skilful the game is, the more players with severe disabilities, respectively 1 and 2 point players, can be successfully included in the game of wheelchair basketball. Adherence to the principle of non-contact allows all players to truly demonstrate their basketball skills.

Consequences for officials who join wheelchair basketball

Involvement in wheelchair basketball means mu more than contributing to the development of sport: The knowledge of the history of wheelcha basketball, its relation to the rehabilitation of pe sons with severe disabilities who literally died bef re the modern treatment of spinal cord injuries w developed by Sir Ludwig Guttmann in 1944 (GUT MANN 1976, 21). The unique experiences human values can strengthen the officials' ow interests and determination.

To serve the sport of wheelchair basketball proper as a referee nowadays demands a long and con plex learning process. The skills learned in runnin basketball are not sufficient and need to be mod fied. Much of wheelchair basketball differs fro running basketball. The goal for a wheelchair ba ketball referee can be defined as follows:

■ *„Officiate the game of wheelchair basketba according to the inner structure of this un que sport and in accordance with the natur sense of the game as perceived by experien ced players".*

Referees train to manoeuvre basketball wheelchairs in Stoke 1989. From left: Isaac Lechtmann, Switzerland; candidate from Finland

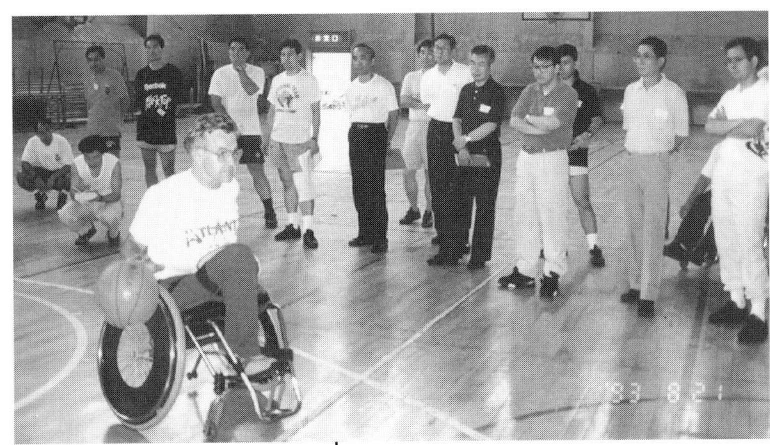

Referees Clinic, Tokorozawa, Japan August 1993: Tip Thiboutot (President Technical Commission IWBF since 1992) demonstrates correct dribbling to Japanese referees

FFICIALS TRAINED IN RUNNING BASKETBALL must re- ›gnize the complexity of wheelchair basketball as ell as the experience, knowledge and proficiency ' its players. The players want to be treated like hletes and not like „the disabled". Players emand that officials recognize wheelchair basket- ıll as a true sport, that they be willing to learn the ›ecific intricacies of the sport and work on its ehalf.

'ARNING THE SPORT of wheelchair basketball is a cru- al issue for someone who does not normally use wheelchair. Some may argue that wheelchair bas- etball is not so different from running basketball, ıat referees with highly trained observation skills ın quickly compensate for lack of experience. It is ıis very error in judgement that prevents many ficials from developing their potential to referee heelchair basketball (see WORTH 1986). Using ıose same observation skills, officials can improve ıeir skills to a greater degree when they have xperienced this sport as a player; therefore, pla- ng wheelchair basketball should be an obligation

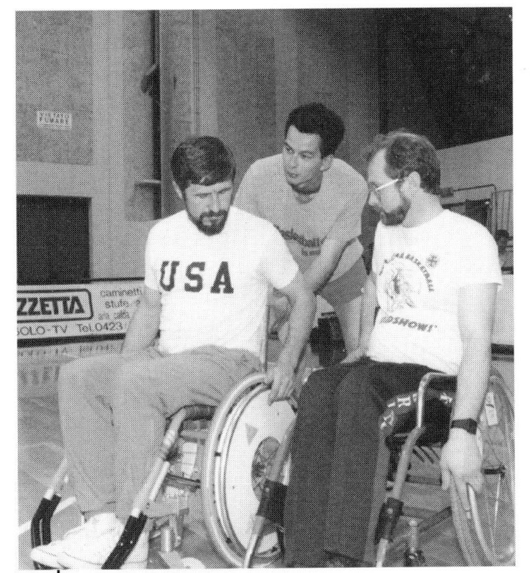

Experts on wheelchair specific fouls: Horst Strohkendl, Norbert Kucera, both Germany; Philip Craven, GB (from left). 1st IWBF clinic on officiating, Treviso, Italy, May 1990

(TONELLO 1991, 134). Officials who have learned to play wheelchair basketball and learned to sense the different qualities of movement of a player in a wheelchair totally support this requirement.

SINCE MANY OFFICIALS and other supporters of the game have learned **to play** wheelchair basketball, the major differences between it and running basketball have become more significant and the interest for specialised information has grown. Modern learning theories stress the necessity of acquiring practical experience in order to develop the skills associated with perception. When observing complex subjects, one can only perceive and assess reasonably when one has experienced and learned those subjects thoroughly. That is why two individuals may differ a great deal when they try to explain what they have observed when watching wheelchair basketball or identifying a foul. Perception of an object includes information obtained from several sensory organs and most of all identifies that object's purpose and its significance. The message becomes quite clear for all persons who are not disabled who wish to officiate wheelchair basketball:

- *Learn to handle a wheelchair; request help from experienced players. They will appreciate the sincerity of your approach.*

- *Learn to play wheelchair basketball. It is much easier to learn than you would expect.*

- *Communicate with players on all wheelchair specific issues and doubtful cases. They also wish to benefit from your expertise on rules.*

Referees at 9th Paralympiad in Barcelona 1992

Referees all over the world: Vlad Eshenko, Gilles Brière, Canada

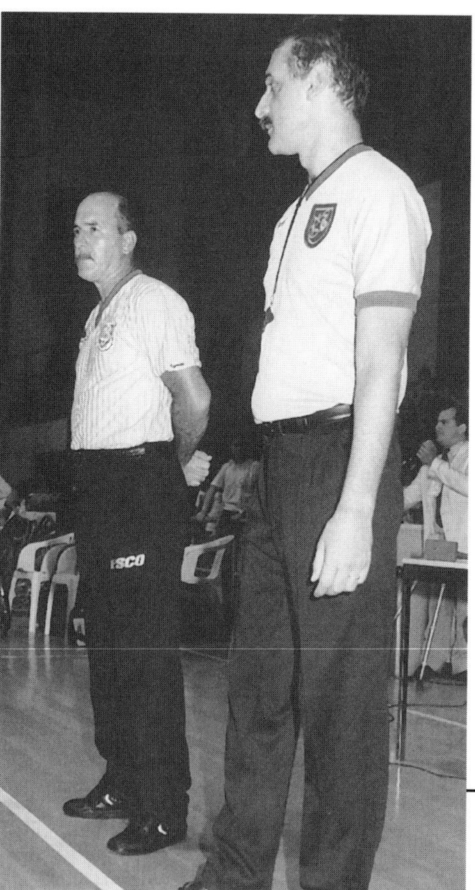

Referees all over the world: Bestilleiros, Argentina (right) and Sergio Castro, Brazil

THE IWBF HAS PROVIDED a curriculum for the traini of wheelchair basketball (see Technical Committ IWBF. Handbook, Section III, 1991) and ju recently a paper on „Positioning of Referees Wheelchair Basketball"(1995). The above arg ments should convince referees and even gui them towards the goal of excellence. The playe are actually waiting to assist and to share comm experiences. Wheelchair basketball can be learn through a combination of acquired experience ar application of existing observation skills; ultimat ly, a stronger identification with this great sport w be established.

Kenji Mizuta, Japan

[M]ajor Rule Differences in Wheelchair Basketball [F]rom Running Basketball*

1973

[A]doption of the liberalized Dribbling Rule (Art 38) and Progressing with the Ball Rule (Art. 39), according to the NWBA model

[A]doption of the NWBA Free Throw (Art 60, C.1): [f]ront wheels (castors) may be in advance of the [l]ine.

[D]ifferent rules between female and male wheelchair basketball have been deleted (smaller ball, [f]ree throw line 1m shorter)

1976

Definition of dimensions of wheelchair and cushion (Art 4 Equipment F).

1982

Adop. of the Player Classification System. (Art. 62).

1984

Adoption of Art. 31 E: An offensive player is only allowed to enter the restricted area during an out-of bounds situation when the ball is in play.

1990

Adoption of „Alternating Process Rule" (Art. 26 B); Change of cushion rule (Art. 4 Fa): 5cm thickness for 3.5, 4 and 4.5 players and 10cm thickness for 1, 1.5, 2, 2.5 and 3-point players; lifting in all cases is a technical foul (Art. 52 i).

1994

Definition of wheelchair specific personal fouls (Art. 47);

3-Second Rule (Art. 40), change from 5-Second Rule.

Definition of a Player in the Act of Shooting (Art. 29);

Player Out-of-Bounds and Ball Out-of-Bounds (Art. 37,4): intentional throwing of the ball against an opponent to obtain a throw-in forbidden.

1994/95

Printed and published the first complete book of wheelchair basketball rules and interpretations, with the assistance of FIBA.

All unnecessary rules such as Art. 44 and regulations concerning pivot or dunk are deleted.

*Rules written in italics are of major significance.

Participants of the 1st IWBF clinic on officiating, Treviso, Italy, May 1990

PLAYER CLASSIFICATION

Classification, the emancipation from the patronage of medical doctors

The game of wheelchair basketball was invented by players with spinal cord injuries. These players were hospitalized for years at Veterans Administration Hospitals in the U.S. in order to successfully complete their rehabilitation. At this stage of development, classification was not an issue of concern. All players were totally „confined" to their wheelchairs. In the USA and later on in many other countries, the problems of classification and eligibility were raised when persons with other disabilities and especially ambulatory persons joined wheelchair basketball as players.

Wheelchair basketball as a means of normalisation in the USA

The classification issue in wheelchair basketball arose in the USA in the early years with the question: Who should be allowed to play? Persons with disabilities other than spinal cord injuries, such as leg amputations and poliomyelitis, joined wheelchair basketball when the first home town teams had been created in the U.S. (Kansas City Pioneers and the New England Clippers in 1947). The attraction of the new sport began to reverse the antipathy of ambulatory persons towards the use of a wheelchair. Many wheelchair basketball players did not use a wheelchair in daily life.

The National Wheelchair Basketball Association (NWBA) regarded itself from the beginning in 1949 as a national sports organization and a necessary complement to the National College Athletic Association (NCAA). The players focused primarily on sports and readily followed Nugent's philosophy of normalization in essence by trying to assimilate the running basketball model and adhering as closely as possible to its rules, players gain maximum benefits. In essence, this philosophy permitted all players to participate who could not successfully play running basketball because of a permanent physical disability of the lower extremities. In 1951, this approach was formulated more precisely as an NWBA rule and to this date has never been challenged:

- „Any individual who because of the severity of his leg disability or the lower portions of the body will benefit through his participation in wheelchair basketball and who would be denied the opportunity to play basketball were it not for wheelchair basketball shall be eligible to play." (LABANOWICH 1988, 14)

This definition and the philosophy of normalization behind it, is the strongest argument advanced thus far for denying the eligibility of able-bodied players for wheelchair basketball. It is the profound conviction of US society that anybody benefits from participation in the sport of basketball by striving for elite performance and by challenging a players physical and mental potential. This challenge is provided for the able-bodied in running basketball, and for persons with disabilities of the lower extremities in wheelchair basketball.

The desire to attain elite performance and the strong belief in human creativity as well as in the players' potential to develop useful compensation skills, for a long time hindered the introduction of a classification system in the NWBA. The need for such a system may have been discussed before 1964, when finally a 3-class system with 13-team balance points was implemented into the official events of the NWBA. The decision was taken by the delegates of the member teams of the NWBA, after it was prepared by a working committee of experts and recommended by the Executive Committee (LABANOWICH 1975, 155-165).

- **Class I**
  Complete spinal paraplegia at T9 or comparab[le] disability where there is a total loss of muscul[ar] function originating at T9 or above.

- **Class II**
  Complete spinal paraplegia at T10 or below [or] comparable disability where there is a total lo[ss] of muscular function originating at T10 an[d] below.

- **Class III**
  All other disabilities (of the legs) with no trun[k] involvement. Team balance points: 13 (LABANOWICH 1975, 157).

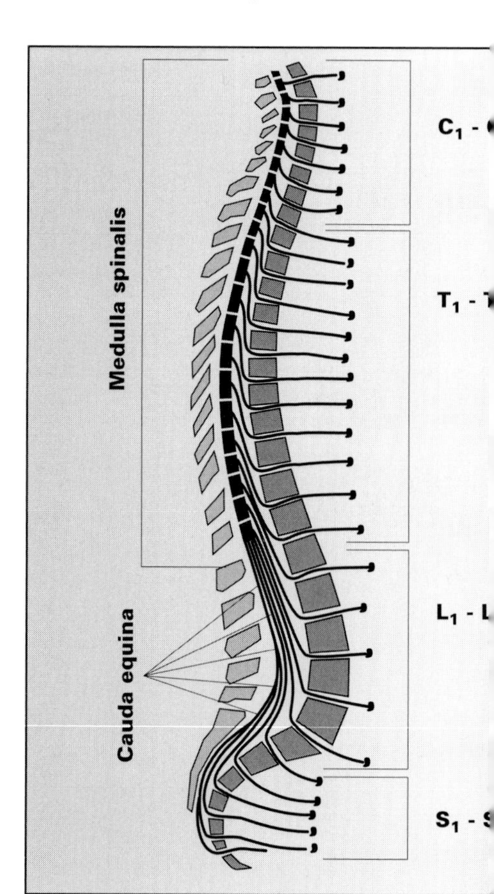

Definition of classes according to th[e] level of the spinal cord lesion

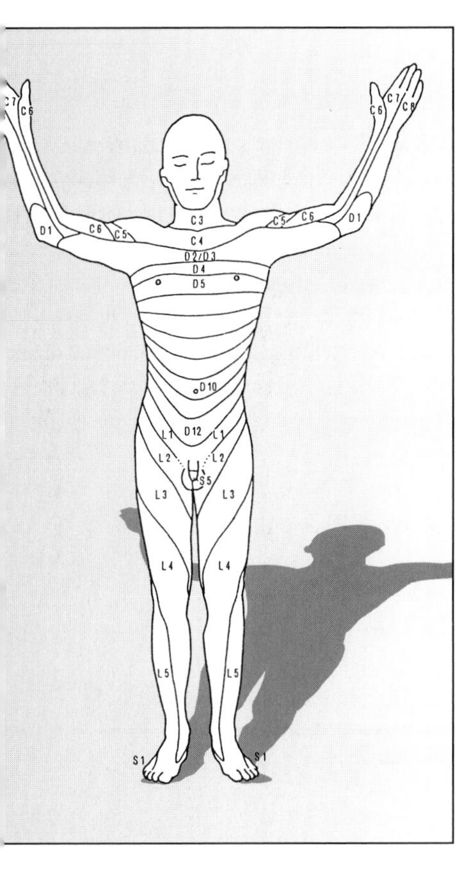

Sensoric innervation of the body

EDICAL CLASSIFICATION ND ITS LIMITATIONS

N CLASSIFICATION MATTERS, the international scenario wheelchair basketball was heavily influenced by representatives of the ISMGF, by Sir Ludwig ttmann and his medical colleagues, dating back 1956 (Labanowich 1988). Classification was st proposed for individual sports and then for eelchair basketball, when players with poliomy- tis became eligible for the International Stoke ndeville Games. Guttmann decided to separate players into two groups, one with complete spi- cord lesions and the other with incomplete le- ns. Players with incomplete lesions consisted stly of players with polio. They were regarded as perior wheelchair basketball players than their unterparts with complete lesions of the spinal cord, not for their greater skills, but because of their greater physical and functional potential. This difference in physical capacity was felt to be so significant that separate and distinct competitions were formed for each group of players. Beginning in 1956, participating countries could enter two basketball teams in two separate competitions at the annual Stoke Mandeville Games.

CONTRARY TO THE NWBA's philosophy, players with disabilities other than neurological impairments, such as amputations of the lower limbs, were not eligible in Stoke Mandeville untill 1986 (LABANOWICH 1988, 39). The strong historical relationship between the treatment of spinal cord injuries and the development of wheelchair sports centered the interest of Guttmann and his medical colleagues solely on those individuals with paraplegia who were *„confined“* to a wheelchair. From the physicians' point of view, these individuals should receive priority in wheelchair sports, for example, wheelchair basketball, where as the ambulatory should choose other sports which were from the physicians' point of view, more appropriate to their disability. This attitude presupposed that the wheelchair could not serve as sports equipment and secondly, that it would prevent ambulatory persons from developing their walking skills. Sports as a means of rehabilitation and a supplement to physiotherapy still prevails in the perception of many people in the medical field, as well as in the perception of many lay persons.

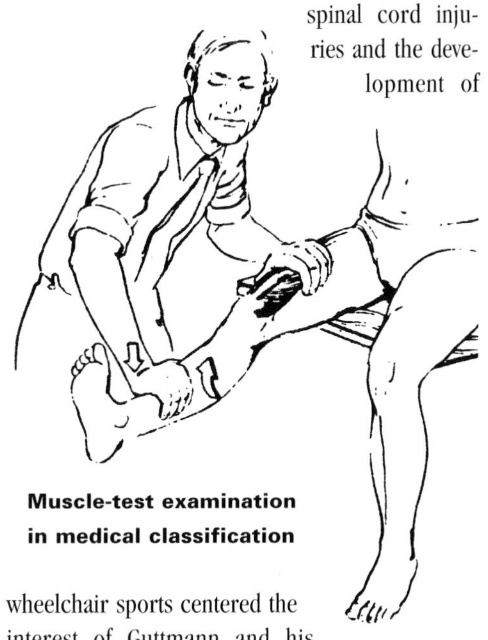

Muscle-test examination in medical classification

THIS APPROACH MINIMIZES the emotional values of physical activities and the mental benefits derived from playing sports. Our bodies and senso-motor systems are the only means with which to cope and to recognize the motivating challenges that are offered by sports, the means to gain maximum pleasure and personal satisfaction. The positive psychological effects resulting from the process of readjustment and from the development of a new identity, represent the major benefits of sports in the rehabilitation of individuals with severe physical disabilities. They help to transcend physical limitations. Improvements in strength, coordination, flexibility and endurance, which are primarily the goals of physical rehabilitation medicine, are part of training programmes that support successful participation in sports.

GUTTMANN AND OTHER medical personnel remained locked into a simple chemo-physical model of man and projected this perception onto sports as well as rehabilitation. Under this assumption, it became not only reasonable to discourage ambulatory persons from using a wheelchair, but to promote those kinds of sports and physical activities which include the impaired body parts into the movements and physical skills, such as sitting volleyball or stand-up table tennis for athletes with leg amputations.

IN ADDITION TO this limited understanding of the benefits of sports, major technical arguments existed to exclude non-paralysed players (amputees, persons with cerebral palsy etc.). Their physical disability was not measurable through neurological methods and therefore not comparable to spinal cord injuries. The medical classifiers were very convinced of their assumption. Having experienced great difficulties in comparing complete and incomplete lesions, how could anyone assume they could classify players with a different disability?

CLASSIFICATION IN 1966, complete and incomplete lesions was combined. This new classification system was not the result of an improvement of an applied neurological method, but of the pressure from the organizers of the Stoke Mandeville Games who could not accomodate two basketball divisions, particularly since more countries were competing and the number of other events had grown significantly. In Tel Aviv in 1968, at the Third Paralympiad, the following classification system was applied (Fig 2), one which certainly had great weaknesses, when we compare the wide range of disabilities within the defined classes and the absence of specific classification criteria related to the sport of wheelchair basketball:

■ **Class A**	T1 - T9 complete	1 point
■ **Class B**	T1 - T9 incomplete	2 points
■ **Class C**	T10 - L2 complete	2 points
■ **Class D**	T10 - L2 incomplete	3 points
■ **Class S**	(Cauda equina par.)	3 points
Team balance points: 12		

Fig. 2 (HUBERMANN 1968)

BEGINNING IN 1969 and until 1973, the above system was modified by a proposal from Dr. Bedwell of Australia. He defined a basic structure of classes according to levels of complete lesions and introduced some basic functional muscle tests that could assist in allocating the incomplete lesions to the appropriate class.

FIG. 3 SHOWS THE medical classification for wheelchair sports and the part relevant to wheelchair basketball. The definition of minimal disability and the question of eligibility was an arbitrary one in the opinion of the affected players; it was not related to the actual opportunity to play basketball, but to the ISMGF policy that presumed that it, the ISMGF, was more responsible for the severely disabled.

ISMGF Classification	**Wheelchair Basketball**
■ **Class Ia, Ib, Ic**	1 point
■ **Class II**	
T1 - T5, no balance	1point
■ **Class III**	
T6 - T10, fair balance	1 point
■ **Class IV**	
T11 - L3, good trunk muscles	2 points
■ **Class V/IV**	
L4 - S2, leg muscles	3 points
Team balance points: 11	

Fig. 3

Cord Level	**Class**	**Characteristics**
C4, C5, C6, C7, C8	IA, IB, IC	**IA** Triceps 0 - 3 **IB** Triceps 4 - 5 wrist flexion and extension may be present **IC** Triceps 4 - 5 wrist flexion and extension present Finger flexion and extension 4 - 5. No useful hand intrinsic muscles
T1, T2, T3, T4, T5	II	No useful abdominals No lower intercostals
T6, T7, T8, T9, T10	III	Upper abdominals (good) No useful lower abdominals No useful lower trunk extensors
T11, T12, L1, L2, L3	IV	Good abdominals and spinal extensors Some hip flexors and adductors Points: 1 - 20 traumatic Points: 1 - 15 polio
L4, L5	V	Points: 21 - 40 traumatic Points: 16 - 35 polio
S1, S4	VI*	Points: 41 - 60 traumatic Points: 36 - 50 polio

Not Eligible
Traumatic 61 points and above/Polio 51 points and above
*Class VI is a "subdivision" of class V aplied in swimming only

IN ORDER TO ARRIVE at a precise differentiation b
ween Class IV and Class V/VI, respectively 2 and
point players in wheelchair basketball, the Da
els/Worthingham muscle strength test was applie
The grade of strength of the 16 major mus
groups of both legs were measured by giving poi
values from 0 through 5. The total points of the
muscle groups determined the class, and therefo
the points of a player and even his/her eligibility:

- **Class IV, 2 points**
  0 - 20 points, paraplegics
  0 - 15 points, poliomyelitis
- **Class V/VI, 3 points**
  21 - 60 points, paraplegics
  16 - 50 points, poliomyelitis
- **Not eligible**
  61 - 80 points, paraplegics
  51 - 80 points, poliomyelitis

Fig. 4

THE ABOVE SYSTEM did not seem to have any scienti
base although some doctors supported its applic
tion (McCANN 1975). Commonly used neurolo
cal tests were applied on an examination tab
behind a curtain, far away from the court. The cla
sifiers could not prevent the players from cheatin
The players' „reasoning" was not always based
gaining an advantage, but to be more fairly clas
fied in comparision with other players. Actually, t
definition of the classes excluded the higher thor
cic lesions and failed to classify the incomplete le
ons properly. The complete spinal cord injur
players felt disadvantaged and became very frustr
ted. All complaints could not be resolved, becau
the medical classification system had no effecti
controls. The system was not wheelchair basketb

Definition of the classes for wheelchair sports in 1974

ecific, not understood by the players and failed to ovide reasonable observation criteria. This tem excluded not only players with physical dis-ilities other than paralysis and paresis, but even ny less disabled persons, whose impairment was nificant but not sufficient to meet the most itrary limits. No one ever gave a rationale to lain the difference between paraplegics and yers with poliomyelitis of 10 muscle strength ints. That difference became manifest on the bas-tball court, a difference that neurological tests led to define.

E DOMINANCE OF the Medical Committee and the plication of a system which possessed only a tant relationship to the parameters defining the abilities of players involved in wheelchair bas-tball caused many frustrations, especially for the raplegics with complete lesions. Feeling to some tent helpless in relation to the powerful Medical mmittee, the players assumed an attitude of resi-ation and consequently remained in an unequi-le position. The bias in the relationship between physicians and the players is highlighted by the k of sensitivity to safeguard their privacy during classification procedure, which is described by layer as follows:

„Having been pricked by pins, probed by the examiner's fingers, and ultimately dehumanized, the player is finally classified, almost always after being both prone and supine on an examination table, subject to the analytic gaze of the classifiers, who are usually standing, literally looking down at the player. Let's face facts: The player here has been reduced to a patient… the basketball player has been deathleticized.“
(THIBOUTOT 1990, 46)

E ABOVE ANALYSIS and assessment of the medical ssification system is in retrospect one of the ny examples in history where a limited or even inaccurate model describing man is considered real, or substitutes a „reality“ in order to meet the needs of a particular scientific interest. False reasoning of this kind not only strips human values from persons with disabilities, but also destroys fair dialogue which normally should be based on mutual respect and appreciation in the fields of sports and rehabilitation. A negative process such as this produces prejudice and ignorance on both sides, especially when one partner, in this case the medical classifier, maintains superiority and political power.

Foundation and Implementation of the Player-Classification-Wheelchair-Basketball

IF WE APPLY THE ANTHROPOLOGIC and pedagogic model of man described by NUGENT (1964), we arrive at a different assessment of persons with disabilities. Nugent demonstrated how the challenges persons with disabilities confront and overcome engender sincere admiration and respect. To Nugent, wheelchair basketball players became models of self-determination as opposed to objects of patronization. This approach has a most encouraging effect on the relationship between persons with and without disabilities. Experiencing and perceiving what great challenges human beings can master, many non-disabled persons will be encouraged to assist persons with disabilities to succeed during a most difficult learning process in rehabilitation.

ACTUALLY, IT WAS THIS BASIC approach that founded a relationship of mutual appreciation between a young scientist of adapted physical education, namely Horst Strohkendl, and wheelchair basketball players with spinal cord injuries in Germany in the year 1969. He listened attentively to the complaints of the players, all affected with complete spinal cord lesions. Their proposals outlining how basketball players should be differentiated into classes formed the fundamental structure of the functional classification system (STROHKENDL 1974). Because of the discrepancy between the assessment of the players and the results of the medical classification system, action was demanded immediately if players with complete spinal cord injuries were to be prevented from dropping out of basketball.

COMPLAINTS ABOUT THE medical classification system were a major issue at each tournament. The Medical Committee discussed changes as well as improvements and appealed to fairness in classification. But only very few players resisted the temptation to try to cheat in order to obtain a more favourable classification. The victims of this cheating were players with complete spinal cord lesions, especially those with high thoracic transections of the spine. Classification in wheelchair sports became associated with cheating, with unfairness and with the basketball related ignorance of the classifiers in charge.

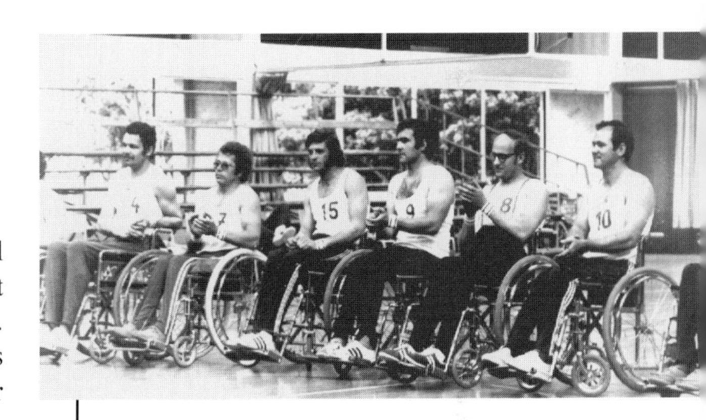

Player of the German National Team 1974, Kerpape, France: They gave the basic information for the development of the functional classification system in wheelchair basketball

THE PROPOSALS OF THE GERMAN male and female players, who were members of the national team in the early 1970s, were empirically examined in 1974/75 and the first results offered to the Medical Committee of the ISMGF in 1976. The final document was published under the title: „Funktionelle Klassifizierung für den Rollstuhlsport“ in 1978. Practical demonstrations followed, which were well received. It was therefore difficult to understand, when one experienced the obvious injustice in classification as a coach and player, why the Medical Committee did not take immediate action. The problems associated with classification were not only manifest in basketball but also in other sports, especially in swimming.

Discussion on classification issues: Armand „Tip“ Thiboutot and Horst Strohkendl (left)

YEARS PASSED BY. Dr. McCann became Chairman of classification in the ISMGF in 1980 and again no action was taken. Under these circumstances it was almost too late when the Subsection Wheelchair Basketball of the ISMGF took the initiative and appointed its own Classification Committee. Another experience from history proved to be true: privileged groups in possession of political power and influence rarely change in response to reasonable proposals and arguments, but change is initiated by another political power that exerts its influence. Stan Labanowich organized international wheelchair basketball according to the democratic and player-oriented system of the NWBA (USA), thereby creating a political environment in which opposition to medical classification could be freely expressed.

IN 1982 IN FALUN, Sweden, the first Classification Committee of the Sub-Section of the ISMGF was appointed to implement the functional system quickly which had by then been ready for six years. The new system was based on movement and skill patterns that are determined by the remaining functional potential of the players using an adapted wheelchair, and the effort required to execute defined basketball skills as effectively as possible according to the objectives and rules of the game. Experienced players sense the effectiveness and quality of each player's action as well as that player's innate physical potential, level of training and talent. Players with thoroughly trained and highly refined observation skills rank the players according to different qualities: skill level, talent, experience, functional potential (STROHKENDL 1991). They assess the players in total (ganzheit) as well as in parts, but always in relation to the purposes of wheelchair basketball.

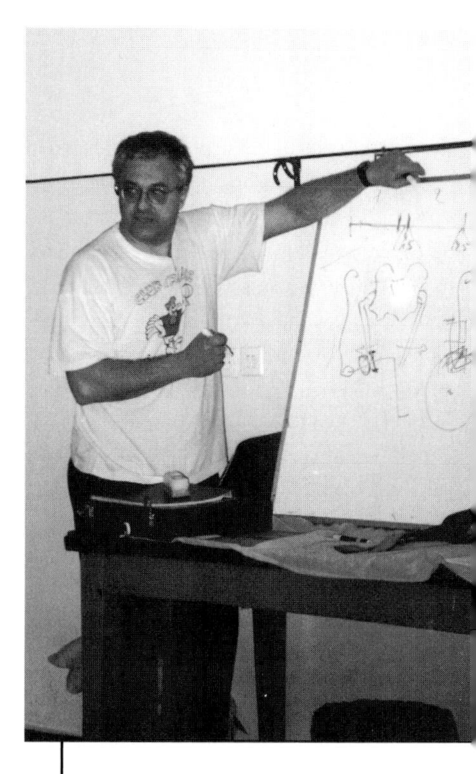

Bernard Courbariaux, since 1988 devoted President of the Classification Commission of the IWBF as tutor in Tehran, I.R. Iran, 1994

IN WHEELCHAIR BASKETBALL and its system of classifi[...] tion the description of these very complex perc[...] tions and images of the players in medical ter[...] constitutes therefore only a small section and a v[...] simple abstract of the entire system:

Class I	above T7	1.0 point
		1.5 points
Class II	T8 - L1	2.0 points
		2.5 points
Class III	L2 - L5	3.0 points
		3.5 points
Class IV	S1 - S2	4.0 points
		4.5 points

Team balance points: 14

Fig. 5

r MEDICALLY TRAINED INDIVIDUALS, the above neurolo-
al parameters provide an initial approach to ssification which must eventually be supplemen- by criteria related to wheelchair basketball. erefore, novices in classification may experience at difficulties or may not even succeed if they ntinue to think and discuss classification solely medical terms and fail to assimilate the observa-

Martina Tschötschel (right) one of the German originators of the classification system during the process to become an international classifier with Bernard Courbariaux

n skills of players. These demands may not con- m to the actual principles and methods of natu- sciences. On the other hand, the question must Are the methods of the natural sciences appro- ate to assess such a complex issue as the physi- potential of wheelchair basketball players? The yer-classification-wheelchair-basketball is an dinal scale that has developed through expe- nce. Any classification system that attempts to antify disability or function has misinterpreted or sunderstood the purpose of classification (see NLANDEWIJK 1995, BRASILE 1990).

MOST PLAYERS ARE UNFAMILIAR with scientific principles and methods. They may even be totally unaware of most medical impairments and their definitions. But they know what is limiting and what is helpful when playing wheelchair basketball (RIDING 1990, 65).Therefore, active players learn much easier by watching typical representatives of the 4 classes. Possessing a profound knowledge to sense the physical potential of the typical player of a class, they also succeed in classifying players with disabilities other than paraplegia and even special cases (e.g. a player missing one hand). The half point options are applied in instances where players actually meet the specific characteristics of two adjacent classes. Players demonstrate flexibility in making difficult assessments, such as assessing players with cerebral palsy.

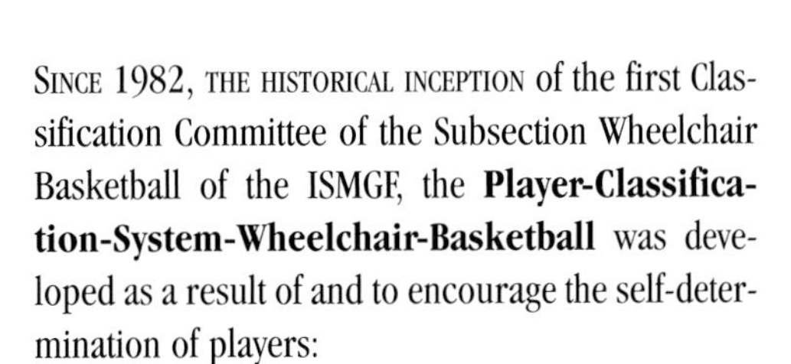

SINCE 1982, THE HISTORICAL INCEPTION of the first Classification Committee of the Subsection Wheelchair Basketball of the ISMGF, the **Player-Classification-System-Wheelchair-Basketball** was developed as a result of and to encourage the self-determination of players:

- All players were informed about the new **four class** system. This task was very easy because it was written, then documented on film, based on the way players perceive and think classification.

- The players learn to assume responsibility for the system by proposing their own classification, controlling the classification of others, or even by functioning as classifiers.

Classifiers and Students at the 6th World Championships in Edmonton, Canada, 1994

- Classification issues are discussed like a playing rule. They should serve the purpose of wheelchair basketball and maintain the high standard of play.

- The classification procedure takes place on court by observation and through fair dialogue. Medical examinations are only exceptionally applied and must be agreed upon by the player. The classification procedure is as simple as possible and always respects privacy.

- The new system includes all players with physical disabilities who wish to play wheelchair basketball and gives everybody a fair chance to reach the highest level of competition.

THE VERY SUCCESSFUL DIALOGUE between experienced players and commited collaborators has led to the creation of a classification system which is generally accepted by the players. For years now, it has ceased to be a major issue at tournaments. The system functions like a language that is learned by experience. If you want to become a classifier, try to play wheelchair basketball and you will, like the players, learn to discriminate between skills and physical function.

Henk Mekkenze (left) at the 6th Paralymiad in Arnhem, the Netherlands 1980

Part Two

EACH DECADE OF WHEELCHAIR BASKETBALL HAS ITS LEGENDS AND BY TAKING THEM IN SEQUENCE, THE READER IS LEFT TO DECIDE WHO IS THE GREATEST OF THEM ALL.

1940's – The game gets underway in the USA and Great Britain

WHEELCHAIR BASKETBALL was invented in the USA by World War II veterans who were former „running" basketball players. There is verbal commentary of the game being played, or at least practised, in 1945 at the Corona Naval Station, California and in Framingham, Massachusetts, two of the many U.S. Veterans Administration Hospitals (VAH).

Coast Guard in the Pacific, was named yesterday as captain of the Boston University football team for 1947.

Villanova; 18, at Harvard; 25, at Syracuse; Nov. 1, at Brown; 8, Colgate; 15, at Columbia; 22, Fordham; 29, at Boston College.

Cushing Wins Over Celtics In Wheel-Chair Basketball

The Boston Celtics last another basketball game yesterday afternoon. And in doing so they proved right the fellow who had said of them after they had dropped several previous contests: "Why, a team in wheel chairs could beat these guys."

A team in wheel chairs did whip the Celtics and badly, too, on the Garden court. It was the disabled war veterans from the Cushing Veterans' Administration hospital at Framingham, who administered the 18-2 defeat. Boston's pro hoopsters for this tussle, likewise rode wheel chairs.

The lads from Cushing, under the direction of Rod Laramie, physical education director at the hospital and former Worcester "Y" swimming coach, took up basketball for diversion and exercise. They ride their wheel-chairs with the same reckless abandon they displayed overseas and have become quite proficient in the court game.

Before the boys took on the Celtics, they scrimmaged among themselves and really put up a lively contest. The way they bumped each other and pushed and grabbed for the ball belied their actual physical condition. Matched against the green-shirted pros they displayed fine teamwork and shooting and except for a blind, overhead toss by Mel Hirsch, would have blanked the Celtics.

"Give us another game," shouted the Celtics.

"Anytime," replied the Cushing boys, but you'd better get some help."

So a return game was scheduled for tomorrow night between the halves of the Celtic-New York Knickerbocker game at the Garden. For reinforcements, the Celtics will have three members of the league-leading New Yorkers to face the wheel-chair demons from Cushing.

Celtics - Framingham, Newspaper December 1946

THE FIRST DOCUMENTED evidence is from 1946. The Flying Wheels of Birmingham, California embark on their first of ten annual cross country exhibition tours. An article from the „Framingham News" of 6th December 1946 records a demonstration match between the players of the Cushing Veterans Hospital, Framingham and the Boston Celtics at the famous Boston Garden. In February 1947, the first recorded match report appears in the „Framingham News" describing on a game between Wards 505 and 507 at the Cushing Hospital with Ward 505 winning 14 v 12. WALTER MAGUIRE cans all 12 points for Ward 507, but a better spread from Ward 505 wins the day.

New Jersey PVA Wheelers versus Brooklyn Whirlaways in 1949 with legendary Al Youakim as referee

Netball at Stoke Mandeville Hospital in 1949

IN GREAT BRITAIN, a form of wheelchair basketball resembling the English game of netball starts to be practised in 1947. It has its origins in 1946 at the Roehampton Rehabilitation Centre near London and is adopted by Sir Ludwig Guttmann's Stoke Mandeville Hospital in 1947 as an ideal team game for wheelchair users. The centre of excellence in the late 1940's is at the Lyme Green Settlement near Macclesfield, Cheshire, England. Here a team of ex servicemen including JIM CHADWICK, JIMMY HOOKER, ARTHUR „SMUDGE" SMITH, RON FOSTER, GEORGE NEWMAN and all-time superstar GEORGE „GINGER" SWINDLEHURST practise with military precision at 3pm every day, sweeping snow off the court in winter.

In 1948, the first home town wheelchair basketball team is founded in the USA, the Kansas City Bulldozers. Lyme Green continue to practise wheelchair netball in preparation for the first national tournament which will take place at Stoke Mandeville the following year.

At the second Stoke Mandeville Games in June 1949, the players from Lyme Green win their first National Games title, a feat they would repeat on eighteen successive occasions in the future. Certain players from these early years are worthy of special mention:

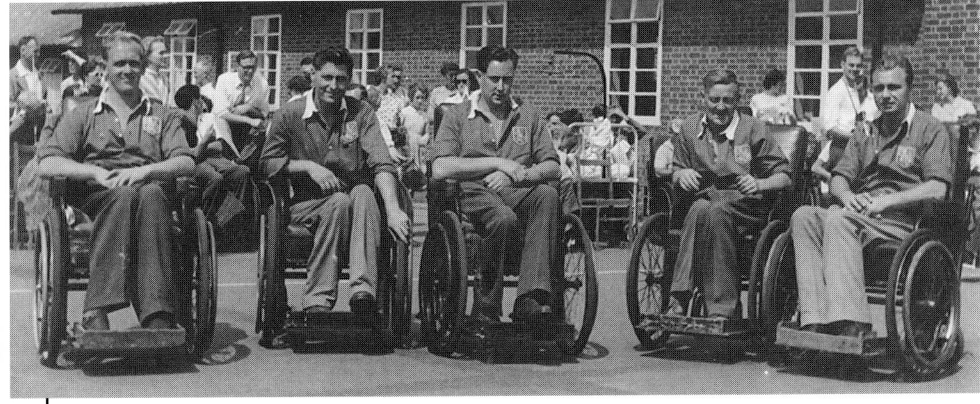

Lyme Green Settlement netball team: George „Ginger" Swindlehurst, Jimmy Hooker, George Newmann, Jim Chadwick, Arthur „Smudge" Smith (from left)

No single organization is responsible for wheelchair basketball in the USA. The game needs a national co-ordinating body which sees the birth, in 1949, of the National Wheelchair Basketball Association (NWBA). The first National Wheelchair Basketball Tournament (NWBT) also takes place that year in Galesburg, Illinois and is won by Kansas City.

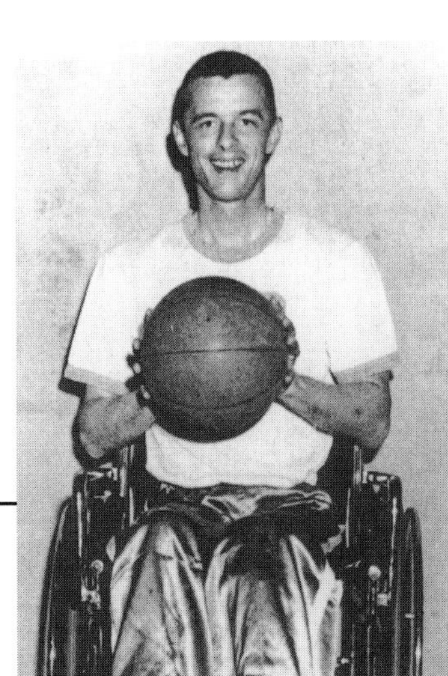

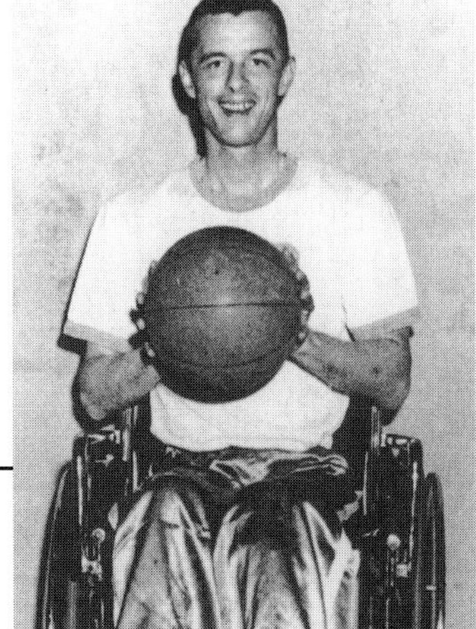

Bill Clem

Robert H. Miller, a player of Kansas City Pioneers, first elected President oft the NWBA in Galesburg, Illinois, 1949

- JACK CHASE – One of the smoothest and swiftest players of all time and holder, over the years, of many NWBA records. He played with the University of Illinois team from 1948 to 1952. He later played with the California Flying Wheels, finishing his career with the Garden Grove Bears of California. A most effective ambassador for the game, he was elected to the All-America team six times.

- BILL CLEM – A player in the first NWBT, as a teenager, and the only person to participate in every national tournament up to 1996 along with founding Commissioner, Timothy Nugent. He perfected the "hook shot" and used it on the freethrow line as well as anywhere on the court. This was partly due to his pattern of paralysis. He was a "heady" and aggressive player, particularly in defence. He played for the Kansas City Bulldozers and was a member of the All-American Team on four occasions.

- BOB MILLER – A founding member of the Kansas City Bulldozers. An outstanding player and leader for many years. He was elected the first President of the NWBA and was an All-American in 1949 and 1950.

- DON SWIFT – One of wheelchair basketball's original participants while a spinal cord injured patient at Hines Veterans Hospital, Chicago in 1946 and 1947. A true leader of men and great organiser of new teams after graduation from college. He was renowned for a unique set shot. He was elected to the All-American Team three times. He died in 1994.

THE 1950'S –THE DAWN OF INTERNATIONAL COMPETITION

IN 1950, ONE OF THE GAME'S great visionaries and advocates of the concept of self-determination for players, TIMOTHY NUGENT, is appointed Technical Adviser to the NWBA. In the same year a third country, Canada, starts to play the game. The Dueck „Powerglides" of Vancouver are founded in 1950 by DOUG MOWAT.

IN 1951, IN THE EAST of Canada, WILLIAM „BILL" HEPBURN encourages the „Montreal Paraplegics" to play the game. After a sports journalist writes of his wonderment following their first game, they are named the „Wheelchair Wonders". 1951 also sees the establishment in the New York/New Jersey area of the Eastern Wheelchair Basketball Association of the NWBA, which includes five teams.

THE FIRST INTERNATIONAL Stoke Mandeville Games take place in 1952. Four Dutch ex-servicemen join their British comrades and take part in the different sports, including wheelchair netball. The first true international match takes place the following year in 1953 when the Dutch team is made up of five players - JOEP DE BEER, J. NIJLAND, FRITS VAN OMMEN, GERARD SIMONS and H. STAAL. Lyme Green represents Great Britain and the „Wheelchair Wonders" compete for Canada.

DURING A RETURN VISIT to the Netherlands in 1953, the Lyme Green team sees that basketball is played with a backboard as well as a ring. Beginning in 1954, the Stoke Mandeville tournament includes backboards. In 1954, the first international exchange of club teams takes place when the „Wheelchair Wonders" are invited to the sixth NWBT in New York City. The New Jersey Wheelers win the title.

BY 1954, TWO NEW PLAYERS have joined the Lyme Green squad: BILL SHIELS, who was initially an archer and PADDY MORAN, a Korean war veteran, who possesses a great outside shot and to whom today's three-point line would have not proved an obstacle to his two-handed set shot.

THE PAN AM JETS of the USA are, undoubtedly, th legends of the 1950's. Sponsored by Pan America Airways they compete for the first time at Stol Mandeville in 1955. Over the next three years, th Jets convince the authorities that wheelchair ba ketball and not wheelchair netball will be the spo that takes the world by storm over the next for years.

THE FIRST RULE that they help change is to make field goal count two points instead of one. They pla the game in Everest and Jennings (E&J) rear whe drive chairs which weigh „only" 24 kilogramme To quote GINGER SWINDLEHURST „The Jet's chai freewheeled in a straight line once having bee pushed, unlike ours and the Dutch front wheel dr ve armchairs which weighed up to 50 kilos an demanded that the hands remain far more on th

The Netherlands' netball team at 1st international tournament in Stoke Mandeville 1953

„Les wheelchair wonders" from Quebec, Canada, in Stoke Mandeville 1953

eels; otherwise the chair would be constantly inning". He also said when asked generally about Jets standard of play – „Oh! You mean the yanks o we were constantly trying and failing to catch".

E DOMINANCE OF THE JETS leads the authorities at ke Mandeville to create two classes of competin from 1956 onwards, completes and incomple. The Jets are placed in the incomplete category most of their players are not paraplegics, but ve been paralysed through polio and have partial vement in their legs.

TER THE SHOCK of the 1955 Stoke Mandeville experence, the Dutch and British players realise that nt wheel drive chairs are a thing of the past. It is Dutch who set about copying and building their n version of the E&J chair, albeit in an unfolding

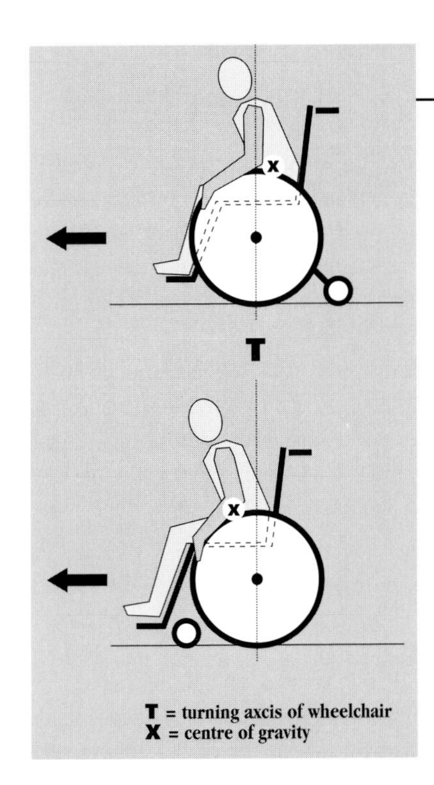

Difference in forward rolling stability

form. GINGER SWINDLEHURST, after visiting the Netherlands for a demonstration match, brings back to Britain one of the Dutch chairs.

SO THE PAN AM JETS confirm wheelchair basketball as the team sport for athletes in wheelchairs. Until the 1990's, many people think that wheelchair basketball was invented at Stoke Mandeville by Sir Ludwig Guttmann. It is easy to see how this misconception grew in credence. Before the arrival of the Pan Am Jets, a form of the game, netball, is already played in Britain. Following the appearance of the Jets at Stoke Mandeville, wheelchair basketball spreads to the rest of the world via Stoke Mandeville and not directly from the USA. Each July, annual scientific meetings coincide with the Stoke Mandeville Games. It is the delegates to these meetings, who having seen wheelchair basketball at the Games, take the game back to their own countries.

The Pan Am Jets in Stoke Mandeville 1955

IN 1955, PHYSIOTHERAPISTS MICHEL BOUBÉE and ALAIN BOSSION introduce wheelchair basketball into their rehabilitation centre at Fontainebleau and the sport begins in France. Great Britain plays a demonstration match against France in Paris in May 1956, winning 14 v 8. The French team then comes to Stoke Mandeville in July 1956 for their first Games. This is the start of a long playing career for LOUIS ARPIN.

DURING THE LATTER PART of the 1950's, wheelchair basketball spreads to Italy, in anticipation of the first Paralympic Games in Rome in 1960. Sweden also takes up the sport under the tutelage of BENGT HÄLLEN. Belgium follows in 1958, introducing two outstanding players in DELOBEL and DESAL.

WHEELCHAIR BASKETBALL starts in Perth, Australia in the mid 1950's and a Western Australian team participates in the 1957 Stoke Mandeville Games. This is the debut onto the international scene of BILL MATHER-BROWN, one of the hardest men ever to shoot a hoop.

THE PAN AM JETS' final contribution to the early development of the game is the realization of the need for properly trained referees. From its inception in 1949 refereeing at Stoke Mandeville has been coordinated by CHARLIE ATKINSON, the Technical Officer of all sports in the Games and a particular fan of wheelchair basketball. He called upon individuals with experience to assist him in refereeing matches at the Games.

DURING THE 1957 incomplete final between the Jets and the Netherlands, Dr. Guttmann disqualifies the Jets for rough play. This is the only „defeat" the Jets suffer in five consecutive appearances at the Stoke Games.

THIS FAMOUS INCIDENT prompts the use, from 1958 onwards, of basketball referees from the RAF Base at nearby Halton, who also help draft the first international rules. The Jets were an all-round team and included in their roster TONY MUCCI, PERCY MABEE, PETE ACCA, DON KENNEDY, MARIO ANTONIO, GUS CONTES, JOHN BASILE, JOE VITTA, ROBERT NOPPER and JOE FOLEY. Special mention needs to be made of their coach JUNIUS KELLOGG as well as players JULIUS JIACOPPO and SAUL WELGER:

- JUNIUS KELLOGG – He was an All-American in college and had played for the Harlem Globetrotters until he became a quadriplegic following a road traffic accident. He returned to sports competition in several activities, but made his mark as the individual who moulded the Jets into an all conquering team.

- JULIUS JIACOPPO – He played with the Brooklyn Whirlaways and the Jets for eighteen years. An extremely strong and fast player with an excellent long shot. He was an All-American four times.

- SAUL WELGER – Started playing in his early teens in the 1940's and though small in size he was big on court. He was a smart, aggressive player, an excellent shooter made the All-American team on nine occasions.

TO CONCLUDE THE 1950'S, it must be stated that in the USA during this period there are some superb players who are never seen on the international circuit until 1960 owing to the monopolisation of the USA entry at the Stoke Mandeville Games by the Pan Am Jets. One of the greatest players ever was BILL JOHNSON (see 1960's for profile). Special mention must also be made of:

- JOHN CHEEVES – An exceptional all-round player, an outstanding shooter and an excellent sportsman. He played for the Long Beach Flying Wheels from 1958 until his unfortunate and untimely death in 1966. He was an All-American in all but one of those years and had already achieved greatness. Had he lived, he would have excelled further and would have been one of the greatest players of all-time.

FROM THE GREAT BRITAIN team special mention has to be made of:

- GINGER SWINDLEHURST, who with Johnson was one of the most complete players to have ever played the game. He had an excellent tactical brain and was a great believer in individual skills training as well as team training. He possessed a deadly outside shot (without quite the range of his team mate PADDY MORAN), was a tireless defender, and showed the mark of a great ballhandler by seeing the defence splitting pass tenths of a second before his teammates or his opponents.
He also was conscious from an early stage in his career of the inequalities and unfairness of the complete and incomplete competition system. He has recently stated that countries entering the complete competition were able to „sli[p] incomplete players into the complete tea[m] owing to the totally ineffective screening (clas[si]fication) system.

1960's – The Paralympic Games and the Start of Women's Wheelchair Basketball

WHEELCHAIR BASKETBALL comes of age in 1960 with th[e] first Paralympic tournaments in Rome. The tourn[a]ments are held outdoors on a compacted san[d] surface and attract six nations in the complete cat[e]gory and ten nations in the incomplete categor[y]. For the first time, the USA brings two nation[al] squads and wins both gold medals. Great Britai[n] continues to be a very strong force in the complet[e] category winning the silver medal. 1960 sees th[e] Netherlands, for the last time for some years, wi[n] the silver medal in the incomplete category.

Court at 1st Paralympiad in Rome, Italy 1960. At the line, 1m in advanc[e] Bill Johnsen

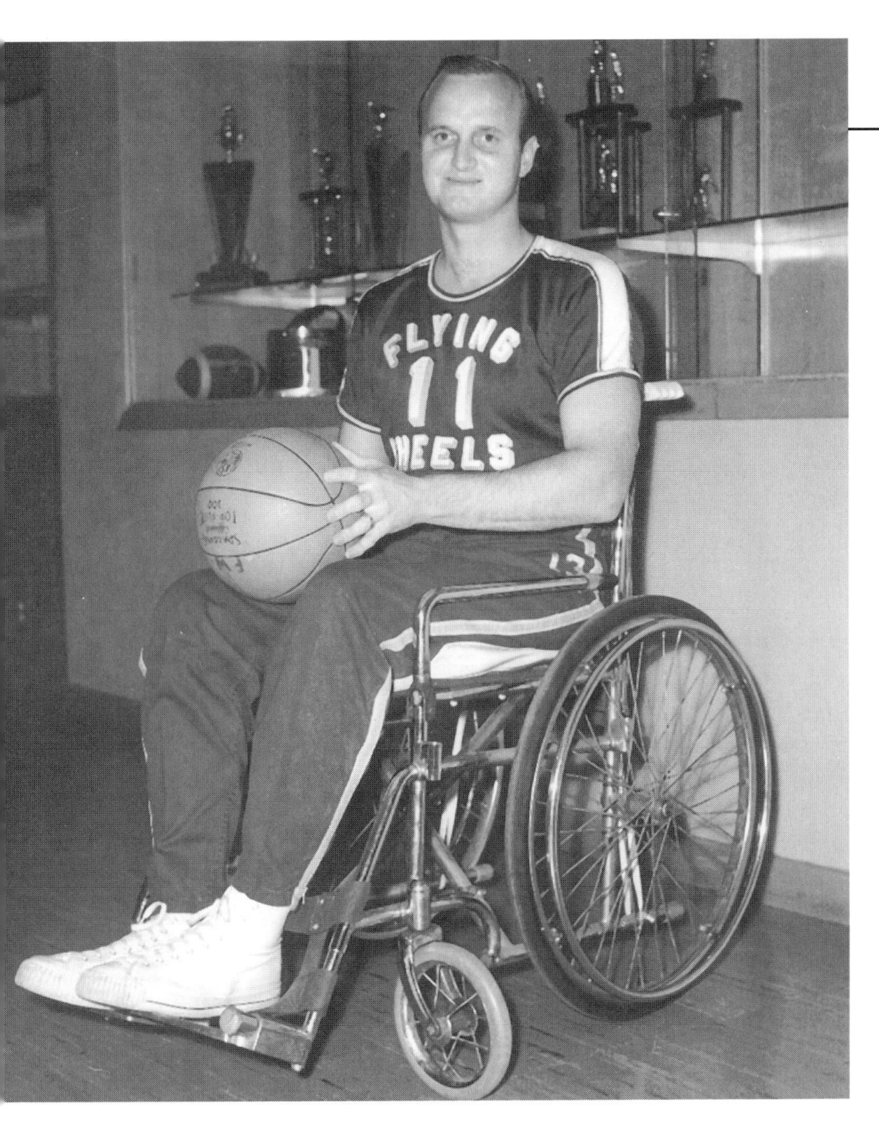

Bill Johnsen

PRIOR TO THE GAMES, host nation Italy makes major efforts to build a competent team. They are most fortunate in possessing one of the best wheelchair athletes the world has ever seen in ROBERTO MARSON. As well as being an outstanding basketball player, he is also a world class track athlete, swimmer and fencer. The Italian team in Rome does not win any medals but will be a dominant force in the incomplete category throughout the early and mid 1960's, winning silver and bronze medals at the Stoke Mandeville Games.

DURING THE EARLY 1960's, certain countries that had started playing the game in the early and mid 1950's do not progress on the international scene. This is particularly due to the existence of very long travel distances in these countries and small concentrations of population which do not permit regular national competition. Countries that are held back by these physical factors are Canada, Australia and Sweden, although each of these nations address these problems in the 1970's.

Team from Victoria, Australia, in 1965

O OF THE US PLAYERS, one from each category, were e legends in 1960:

- BILL JOHNSON – The star of the US complete team was an outstanding and very tough competitor. He started his career with the Long Beach Flying Wheels in 1954, but had to wait until the Rome Paralympics to make the US team. He had a great outside shot and, on top of that, he was the Bob Cousy of wheelchair basketball, or it could be said that Bob Cousy was the Bill Johnson of „running" basketball. He was a master of the look-away and behind-the-back passes and made the All-American team eleven times. He was undoubtedly, one of wheelchair basketball's greatest ever players. It is sad to mourn his passing in 1996.

- RON STEIN – He was the star of the US incomplete side and was also a great track and field athlete. An international news release stated just after the Games that „the greatest athlete in the world could be competing from a wheelchair". He was elected to the All-American team five times. While at college he played for the University of Illinois (1957 to 1960) and finished his career with the St. Louis Rams.

Marvin „Marvellous" Lapicola holds position against Loral „Bud" Rumple

DESPITE GEOGRAPHICAL BARRIERS, Perth in Western Australia stages the first British Commonwealth Games wheelchair basketball tournament in 1962 with Australia winning gold. The Australian team includes BILL MATHER-BROWN, FRANK PONTA and BRUNO MORETTI.

1960 SEES THE START of wheelchair basketball in Israel and the beginning of the career of the greatest player to have ever played the game. BARUCH HAGAI represents his country at the tender age of 15. His contribution in these early years galvanizes Israel into winning the bronze medal in the complete and incomplete categories at the second Paralympic Games in Tokyo in 1964. These results lay the foundation stones for Israel's prominence in international wheelchair basketball over the next 20 years.

IN TOKYO, THE USA again wins both gold medals and another American player hits the headlines:

- MARVIN LAPICOLA – one of the few top flight international players who could rival Bill Mather-Brown of Australia for his relentless and aggressive defensive play.

IN THE INCOMPLETE CATEGORY in Tokyo, a new star, ED OWEN, bursts onto the international scene for the USA. He will continue to dominate for the USA until the 1988 Paralympics in Seoul.

BY THE EARLY 1960's, wheelchair basketball is being played in South America. Argentina, through the work of HECTOR RAMIREZ, starts to produce some remarkable players. In Tokyo, their incomplete team gains second place behind the USA and along with Israel, Argentina is the first nation to put serious effort into the development of women's wheelchair basketball.

1966 SEES SIGNIFICANT changes with the complete and incomplete categories being combined into a composite medical classification system. That year, the second British Commonwealth Games wheelchair basketball tournament takes place in Kingston, Jamaica with England taking its revenge over the Australians.

IN 1967, ISRAEL wins the Stoke Mandeville Games tournament for the first time beating Italy in the final with the USA placing 3rd. The USA wins the first Pan American Games in Winnipeg, Canada. Will Israel repeat its feat of the previous year when the 1968 Paralympic Games are organized on the outdoor court at the Spivak Centre in Tel Aviv?

THIS IS THE FIRST TIME that a women's tournament has taken place and Israel beat Argentina in the final. The USA places third. This tournament sees the start of the illustrious and long career of ZIPPORAH RUBIN who goes on to compete in six consecutive Paralympiads for Israel.

IN THE MEN'S PARALYMPIC TOURNAMENT, five teams are in with a shout for the medals: Argentina, France, Great Britain, Israel and the USA. It will be BI JOHNSON's last starting role in the Paralymp Games. He has great height and speed along si him with ED OWEN and KIM POLLOCK. Argentin maestro, JORGE DIZ in one of the matches incur lifting foul when his quick silver reactions ca him to partially fold his E&J chair while in moti

Zipporah Rubin-Rosenberg 1964, participated since 1964 in 8 paralympiads

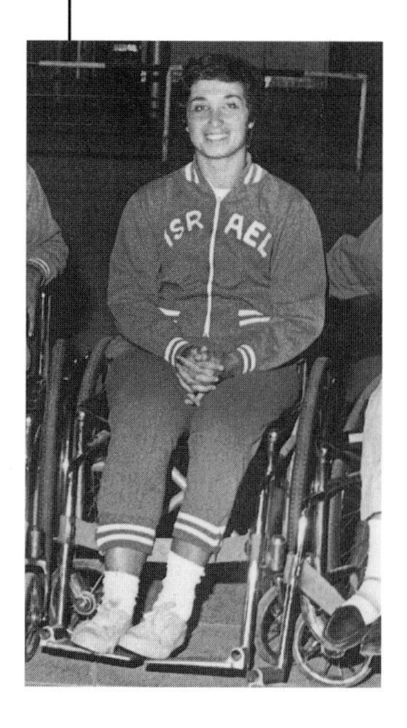

Israel's team in 1967 with Baruch Hagai (left)

Robert Perri, the father of the French wheelchair basketball

·order to get through a gap and hit the lay-up. ›at Britain, for the first time at the Paralympic ·nes, are able to combine their renowned com- te players with incomplete players CYRIL THO- .S, RUSS SCOTT, CARL HEPPLE and rookie ‹RRY KINSELLA. ROBERT PERRI coaches France the first time and, as a result, they have impro- l to a point where they stand a real chance of a ·alympic medal.

ıS THE ISRAELI TEAM coached by REUVEN HELLER 1 led by BARUCH HAGAI and DANNY SHAHAR t overcome the USA in the final, 47 v 37, by using ·at pressure defence and the fast break to nullify US height advantage. Israel has arrived with a ıg, scooping both gold medals.

TEL AVIV, despite finishing fourth behind Great tain, France announces the start of their long ırney toward domination in Europe in the 80's. During the early and mid 1960's, France ıys mainly in continental Europe against the therlands, Belgium, Italy, Germany, Austria, Swit- land and Sweden. In 1965, the French complete egory team defeats the USA in Fontainebleau 26 5. Throughout this period, LOUIS ARPIN, GILLES RDENAVE, RENÉ DAVID, ARTHUR VIGON and ıRCEL BARBIER are the mainstays of the team. It BARBIER who realizes the technical and tactical ortcomings of the French squad and who proaches ROBERT PERRI to become coach in 68.

THE USA in the late 1960's, there are some legen- ry players competing in the NWBA. But for selec- n reasons or, for the simple fact that amputees › not allowed into international competition until Gold Cup in Halifax in 1983, these players are ver seen in a US jersey:

TOM BROWN – One of the fastest and most versatile men ever to play wheelchair basketball. He could shoot from anywhere on court and had a brilliant scoop shot that he could spin off the backboard into the basket from distances of up to three metres. Six NWBT shooting records set by BROWN in 1968 and 1969 still hold good in 1996 (e.g. single game scoring record of 39 points, including 17 successful foul shots while playing for the University of Illinois). He made the All-American team five times.

- ROGER DAVIS – Music City's (Nashville, Tennessee) great player whose outstanding marksmanship and passing were only matched by his fair and intelligent play. Among his many outstanding shooting achievements, he holds the NWBT record for the highest free throw percentage (10 for 10).

- LORAL „BUD" RUMPLE – An outstanding point guard and defensive player. His aggressive play and coaching tactics led Detroit Sparks to seven US championships from 1967 to 1982. He holds the record for the most number of field goals (18) in a NWBT (each team only plays two matches in the NWBT finals). BUD RUMPLE, along with a team supporter JOSEPH JONES, was also responsible for the development of the revolutionary „box frame" aluminium wheelchair in the late 1960's. This chair weighed approximately 16 kilos and was the forerunner of all the non-folding high performance basketball chairs of the 1990's.

The USA team at the 3rd Paralympiad in Tel Aviv, Israel 1968: Bill Johnsen, Ed Owen (No. 40), Denver Branum and Bruce Karr (from left)

As the 1960's comes to a close, Israel reasserts its dominance on the international scene by winning the Stoke Mandeville Games tournament for men, with France placing second, the USA third and Great Britain fourth. PHILIP CRAVEN makes his international debut at the Games scoring 30 points in his first match against Spain.

1970's – New Teams and New Tournaments

Wheelchair basketball specific international tournaments begin in 1970. Until this time wheelchair basketball has always formed part of multi-sports competitions, for example the Paralympic Games, the Stoke Mandeville Games and the Pan American Games.

The first men's European Championship takes place in Bruges, Belgium in May 1970. It is the brain child of ANDRÉ RAES, a Belgian army officer and great fan of the game. Belgium beats France in the final and is led by a highly talented, powerful shooting forward, ANDRÉ ALLEMEERSCH.

The creation of the European Championship expands the number of available tournaments for international teams and causes Stoke Mandeville to rethink the format of its Games. In 1971, a men's second division is added to the Stoke Mandeville Games. This second division competition, which will take place every year apart from 1976 and 1980 up until 1983, gives additional opportunities to the following countries: Sweden, Germany, Spain, Canada, Portugal, Brazil, Italy, Japan, Australia, South Africa, Belgium, Mexico, Denmark, Austria and Switzerland.

From 1970-1975 three teams monopolize the medals in the men's first division at Stoke Mandeville and in the Paralympic Games. These are Argentina, Israel and the USA.

The greatest men's tournament of those years occurs, undoubtedly, at the Heidelberg Paralympic Games in 1972. Great Britain and France, the top two teams in Europe, finish in 4th and 5th positions respectively, but the top three are in a class of their own. Israel defeats Argentina to gain its berth in the final and the USA brushes past Great Britain to set up a battle of the titans. The final is possibly the greatest game ever seen. The Israelis have retained the team that won gold in Tel Aviv, four years earlier. This team has refined its play with further victories at Stoke Mandeville in 1969 and 1971. The USA has individual players who, on paper, are at least the equal if not better than their Israeli counterparts, but will they be able to put it together as a team?

Early in the second half, Isreal threatens to pull away but brilliant 1 on 1 defence by DENVER BRANUM of the USA against the world's greatest player, BARUCH HAGAI, keeps the States in the match. Despite this close attention, HAGAI still drains eight consecutive outside shots. BRANUM fouls out with several minutes left to play. With 13 seconds left on the clock, the Israelis hold a 3 point lead 58 v 55. Enter centre stage, ED OWEN, to sink, what would be today, a 3-point shot as he heads for the left, front corner of the court. When Israel inbounds the ball, OWEN intercepts the pass and with 4 seconds left on the clock puts a 4-foot shot through the hoop as HAGAI tries to stand on his footplates in an effort to check the shot. Israel still manages to get a fast break under way but misses the shot and the USA wins the narrowest of victories 59 v 58.

What of these three great players mentioned in the match report:

- DENVER BRANUM – Another product of the Detroit Sparks team and one of the games greatest defensive players, who could shut down all but the most talented opponent. A great athlete, both on the track and in the pool, he had incredible speed and stamina which permitted him to

Denver Branum

expend twice as much energy as any other p yer on court. He was also extremely dangerc on the fast break and his trademark was a rig handed spin lay-up which started by his toe na and ripped its way through the net by way of top right-hand corner of the back board. last international appearance was at the G Cup, Tampa, Florida in 1979 where, again, won gold.

- BARUCH HAGAI – Why was he possibly the gr test ever player? Baruch had contracted polio a very early age and although an instinct sportsman, he could not participate in „sta up" sports at his school. At the age of 12 came to the Israel Sports Centre for the Disabl in Ramat-Gan and started playing basketb table tennis and swimming, five hours a d seven days a week. At fifteen, he was in the Is eli basketball team. From 1964, he won Paralympic Games table tennis singles title four successive occasions, showing the sa profound tactical awareness that was so app rent on the basketball court. Frequently, more natural talent that a sportsman or spor woman possesses, the less training that indi

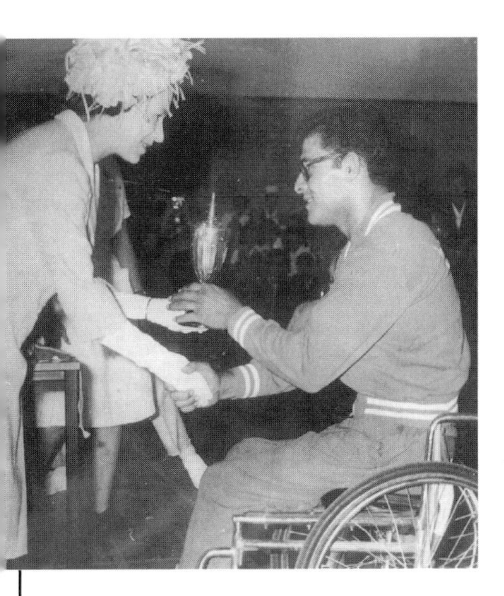

Baruch Hagai and Queen Elisabeth

Denver Branum and Ed Owen

Baruch Hagai, Ed Owen, Moshe Levi, Israel

dual puts into skills and team training. Highly talented individuals sometimes feel that they only need to turn-up and play. This is not the case with the greatest players who consistently produce top-drawer performances. Each sport in the world might only have three, four or five of these individuals who stand out head and shoulders above the rest of the pack. BARUCH HAGAI was at the head of this exclusive pack. Athletic, incredibly skilful and a supreme tactician, BARUCH was such a dangerous player that teams had to double-team him, providing openings to the other highly talented players in the Israeli team. Throughout his international career of 224 matches, he averaged 21 points per match. When his club career is combined with his international career he amassed 19,558 points, 10,236 rebounds and 6824 assists and led Israel to two Paralympic Games titles (1968 & 1980), one World Championship (1975) and three European Championships (1977, 1978 & 1981).

ED OWEN – The consummate fundamentalist and model of sportsmanship. At over two metres, he was one of the tallest men to ever play the game, but he possessed a very rare feature in big men: he thought the game like a 1.70 metre point guard. As a result, he became a complete player, a master of wheelchair handling and positioning and a master of all the ball skills. At the Heidelberg Paralympic Games, German TV was so entranced by OWEN's skills that they filmed him for nearly 30 minutes, during which time ED hardly missed a shot. ED OWEN wrote a text book on wheelchair basketball, demonstrating how the game can be broken down into its constituent parts. ED OWEN dealt in centimetres when discussing wheelchair positioning in order to set a pick and roll. He made the All-American team ten times and led in the organization of several teams and conferences in the USA. At the end of his international career, ED OWEN moved to Germany to spread his vast knowledge of skills to many European countries, especially to women's wheelchair basketball in Germany.

Israel's National team in 1982

THE SECOND WOMEN'S Paralympic tournament also takes place at the1972 Heidelberg Games. Argentina beats surprise finalists Jamaica 28 v 25 with 1968 gold medal winners Israel picking up the bronze medal. The Argentinian team is led by three

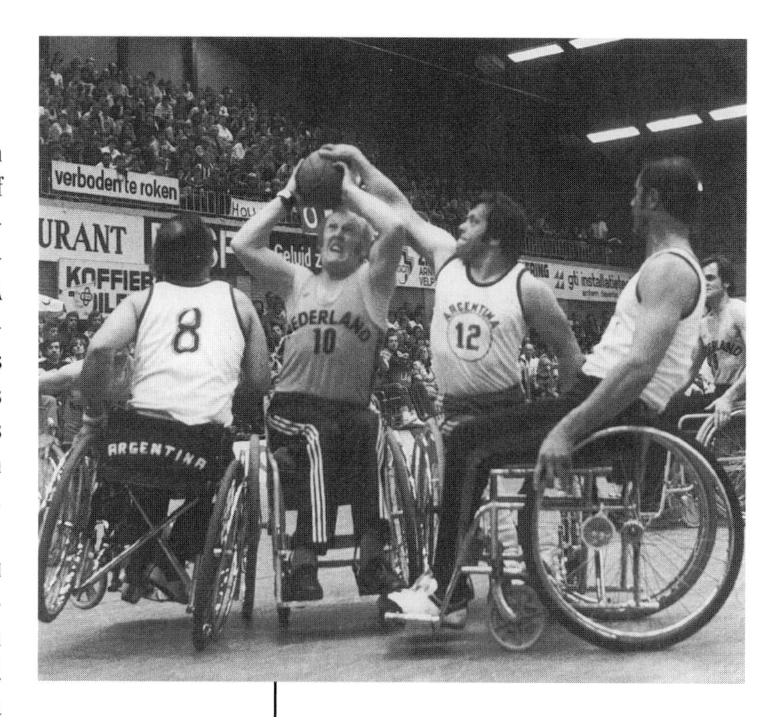

Ad Leyten, the Netherlands, Luis Grieb, No. 12 Argentina, Hector Leurino (right)

excellent players from the early years of women's basketball: SILVIA COCHETTI, GRACIELA DESIMONE and SILVIA TEDESCO. The Heidelberg tournament does not produce any medals for the German women's team, but starts them on their rapid rise to the top.

THE ARGENTINIAN MEN'S TEAM wins the Stoke Mandeville Games first division gold medal in 1973 and 1974. The team has a great „2-1-2" defence marshalled by HECTOR LEURINO and includes defensive towers LUIS GRIEB and ALBERTO PARODI. Two players stand out in this team:

- JOSE LUIS CONSTANTINI – One of the game's most phenomenal shooters, a one-point player who could score from anywhere, with a technically perfect one handed action. He was also extremely dangerous on the fast break, playing at times only token defence. Argentina frequently played four against five in defence, which allowed JOSE LUIS to break early and receive a javelin pass to sink the lay-up.

- HECTOR LEURINO – He dominated the Argentinian „2-1-2" defence and even though Baruch Hagai was known for his constant verbal communication on court, Hector was probably the games most reknown defensive communicator. His trade mark skill was a two handed finger roll lay-up which started by his toes and sneaked over the ring from in front of the basket. He was an extremely quick thinker. In the 1973 Stoke Mandeville final against Israel, the Israelis, in a last gasp effort, had a tight full-court press on the Argentinians. With five seconds remain on the clock HECTOR was in possession of ball and, in order to play out time, he rolled ball to the far corner of the court in Isra defensive half. As the ball reached the corr the final buzzer rang.

Gerry Kinsella in 1976

THE SECOND MEN'S European Championship ta place in Kerpape, Brittany, France in May 19 Great Britain beats France in the final. The Bri team is the strongest seen to that date. At shoo guard is JOHN YOUNG, an immensely strong pla with a highly accurate low-trajectory outside sh The centre is CYRIL THOMAS, the power forwar GERRY KINSELLA, the shooting guard and the p maker is PHIL CRAVEN. GINGER SWINDLEHUR in the twilight of his career, completes the first fi

- GERRY KINSELLA – In 1971, at 23 years of and a club team mate of Phil Craven at Sou port, he already possessed a chess mast knowledge of the game. He understood fro very early age the fundamental importance the pick and roll in order to gain a man adv tage, was a brilliant defender and possessed a lity to score time and again with the most unc ventional shots. An individual of great integr he became a passionate advocate of fairness classification, a very rare feature of players the 1970's. In 1971 at Kerpape, the medi „experts" told him that he should be a two-po player rather than a three-point player. He t the classifiers that if he was a two-point pla he would not play as this would give him unfair advantage over the other players in t category. He remained a 3-point player to end of his career. GERRY's career proved sho lived, when in 1976, he crossed swords with Ludwig Guttmann over the competence of current GB coach and was banned from int national competition in 1977. He never ret ned to the GB team as he had vowed that would not return unless he received an apol from Sir Ludwig.

PHIL CRAVEN (by Armand „Tip“ Thlboutot) – Possibly the greatest one-point player to play the game. A player who could play with or against anyone. A fierce competitor, an outstanding defender and perimeter shooter, as well as a highly skilled ballhandler and student of the game. He constantly tried to develop skills that were not normally practised by one-pointers. In 1972 - 1974, he spent two seasons in France and developed his equivalent of „running“ basketball's lean-away jump shot by fixing his rib cage against the left backpost of his chair and shooting from behind (on top of) the head. This shot became a main part of his offensive arsenal. It was used to deadly and winning effect against the USA in the semi-final of the 1986 Stoke Mandeville Games when he scored 26 points out of Great Britain's 65 points total.
Like teammate Gerry Kinsella, he could never keep his mouth shut in the face of injustice or mediocrity. In a separate incident, to the one in wich Kinsella was involved in 1976, Craven criticized the GB basketball coach and was promptly banned by Sir Ludwig Guttmann. Unlike Kinsella, he accepted an invitation to come back into international competition in 1978. He assumed the role of gadfly, tormenting traditional and tyrannical administrators of wheelchair sports. Later, he relentlessly and successfully, along with Horst Strohkendl, advocated change in the classification process. When he finally hung up his international boots in 1993, he had played 188 times for Great Britain, winning two European Championships, one Gold Cup and one Commonwealth Championship.

…AYED AGAINST GREAT BRITAIN are the pride of Robert …ri's French team. At power forward is GERARD …AZOT, the small forward is MICHEL LE DOZE, … shooting guards are CHRISTIAN ROUSSEL and …N-LOUIS BOILOT. Captain is the playmaker …RCEL BARBIER.

Philip Craven at training 1976, the master of basic skills

- GERARD CHAZOT – The key player, responsible for the French team's major strides forward in the late 1960's and early 1970's. Very fast on court, he possessed great intelligence which he used to exploit the slightest weakness in his opponent. He was an excellent shooter both underneath and around the perimeter of the key. In the many battles between Great Britain and France in the early 1970's, the British knew that if they could restrict France to a ten-point lead at half time, GB would have a good chance to overhaul them in the second half. This was owing to GERARD tiring in the second half. It transpired that he had a heart abnormality which was the cause of his early death in the 1980's. Had CHAZOT's abnormality not been present, the record of matches between the two countries might have been very different.

- MICHEL LE DOZE – a very powerful and combative player whose strength, on occasion, permitted him to make superhuman efforts on behalf of his team. He was a winner through and through and a tremendous leader of men, the perfect foil for Gerard Chazot's more fluid style of play.

IN 1973 ANDRÉ RAES again tries to launch a new tournament, the Gold Cup, also known as the Men's World Championship. The tournament takes place in Bruges, Belgium in April 1973 but Sir Ludwig Guttmann again intervenes in the progress of wheelchair basketball by banning the participation of all non-European teams. Great Britain again beats France in the final of the first Gold Cup and ANDRÉ RAES has to wait until 1975, in Bruges, for the first true world championship to take place.

IN 1974 THE THIRD Men's European Championship takes place in Kerpape, France. Great Britain retains its title, but this time in a very closely fought final against the up and coming Dutch side, captained by one of the greatest players to have ever lived, HENK MAKKENZE. The British team has a new star

Mike McCreadie with Gerry Kinsella

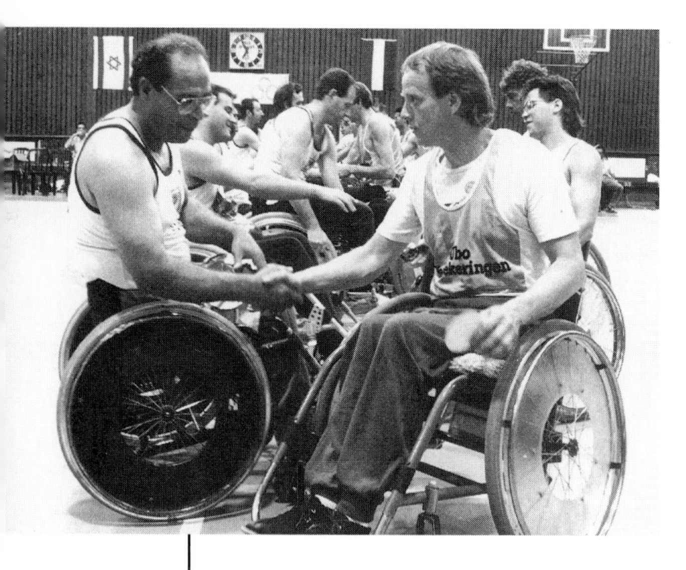

Baruch Hagai and Henk Makkenze, the Netherlands: masters of court control

player in MICK MCCREADIE. The Dutch team includes veterans LEO VAN EIJK and PIET VAN LEEUWEN, shooting guard HUIB KOEKOEK, who possesses one of the most statuesque, upright follow-throughs ever to be seen in the game, and future shooting star FRITS WIEGMANN.

Huib KoeKoek, the Netherlands

THE FIRST WOMEN'S European Championship takes place in conjunction with the men's championship in Kerpape. Germany gains its first gold medal against France in the final. Yugoslavia, in their second appearance in international competition, wins the bronze medal.

THE GERMAN TEAM HAS some exceptional players, amongst them REGINA ISECKE at guard. However, the engine room of the team, coached by HORST STROHKENDL, is occupied by the two Rita's:

- RITA BREUER – playmaker, forward and fast break specialist, she was in a class of her own and was the main reason for the German team scoring so many points, at a time when women's teams averaged 20 to 25 points per match. Rita had excellent shooting mechanics and quickly understood the use of the pick and roll to obtain uncontested lay-ups. She played for Cologne in the German league and many men underestimated her abilities. When a woman has executed a perfect forward for guard pick and roll and then has accelerated into the key to cann a perfectly positioned and executed lay-up, men soon realize that women's wheelchair basketball is serious stuff.

- RITA LAUX – point guard as well as dominant defensive and offensive rebounder. The boards were kept under German control by this quiet but inspirational player who combined with Rita Breuer to form an irrepressible duo.

AT THE STOKE MANDEVILLE GAMES in 1975, Israel wins the gold medal in the men's first division competition. The USA takes the silver and Argentina the bronze. This tournament takes place at the end July. Most of the teams, with Argentina and Fra as the exceptions, travel directly from Stoke M deville to Bruges, Belgium for the first men's wo championship, the second Gold Cup.

Philip Craven with his great opponent in his category, Leo van Eijk, the Netherlands

German women in Kerpape 1974: (from left) Mar Tschötschel, Rita Breuer, Regina Isecke, Rita Lau

ESE TWO TOURNAMENTS in 1975 see the appearance the first time on the international stage of two eat players from the USA, DAVID EFFERSON, a stling speedy guard, and DAVID KILEY probably world's most talented player ever, and unubtedly the USA's greatest ballhandler.

BRUGES, ISRAEL repeats the feat it had performed Stoke Mandeville the week before and beats the A in the final 50 v 47. HAGAI is, not unexpected- in inspirational form but the final baskets are ored by RUBIN. Great Britain defeats the Nether- ds for the bronze medal, the last time they would hieve this feat for twenty years.

THE WOMEN'S TOURNAMENT at Stoke Mandeville in 75, Germany confirms its position as number e in the world by defeating both Israel and gentina for the gold medal. The scene is now set a battle royal at the fifth Paralympic Games to e place in Toronto Canada in August 1976. The German women's team arrive in Toronto as firm favourites for the gold medal. An inspired performance by Israel's point guard ARIELA COHEN MIZAN spoils the party for Germany. Israel wins the final 39 v 32 with Argentina taking the bronze medal. In the men's competition there are over twenty teams entered. DAVID KILEY and ED OWEN, at the top of his form, combine in the final for the USA to comprehensively beat the Israelis 59 v 46. France take the bronze, its first Paralympic medal.

David Kiley: „If you cannot stand up, you must stand out!"

- DAVID KILEY – was the epitomy of the California athlete when he arrived at Stoke Mandeville in 1975, with a deep tan and long sun-bleached hair. It was obvious that here was a very special basketball player, an excellent long-range shooter, penetrator to the basket, a relentless defender and phenomenal passer. The basketball as it passed through the ring for one of his legion three point successes was once likened by an American commentator to a snowflake carressing the net. Author of two of the greatest passes ever seen by one veteran US observer, who noted that he once saved a ball from going out-of-bounds in the backcourt at the foul line extended and simultaneously fired a behind-the-back pass to Curtis Bell who caught the ball just short of the foul line at the opposite end of the court. One week later, against Great Britain at the 1986 World Championship in Melbourne, he replicated this play, but this time from a slightly longer distance. On court he had „on board computer" knowledge of the position of each of his teammates and of the opposition, as well as where their next move. On the international scene, KILEY was always aware of his position as the world's number one ballhandler. Whenever he came up against, as he would view it, a pretender to his throne there would always be a cameo „one on one" contest within the overall match. This occurred on several occasions against Baruch Hagai, Henk Makkenze, Michel Gradelle and Gert-Jan van der Linden, with KILEY coming out on top on most occasions but not always, particularly towards the end of his career. In his international career, he won two Paralympic Games gold medals (1976 and 1988) and three world championship rings (1979, 1983 and 1986). In the NWBA, he combined with Curtis Bell to win eight NWBT titles for the Casa Colina Condors, picking up six Most Valuabie Player (MVP) awards on the way. Undoubtedly one of the greatest players of all time even if his impetuosity, on occasions, could get the better of him.

David Kiley, USA, in typical control of the ball

THE 1976 PARALYMPIC GAMES proves to be a watershed in the fortune of several of the former top wheelchair basketball nations, in both the men's and women's competitions. The Argentinian and British positions in the world standings decline rapidly in the late 1970's. Their places are taken by France, the Netherlands and Sweden. In women's basketball the all conquering Israeli team gives way to an eleven-year domination by Germany who will never lose a major competition until the 1988 Seoul Paralympic Games.

1976 ALSO SEES THE START of the West European League competition for club teams, the forerunner of the Eurocup and Andre Vergauwen Cup competitions. The competition is the brain child of HANS TUKKER, future President of the IWBF European Zone, who is ably supported by WILLI BRINKMANN of Germany and ANDRÉ VERGAUWEN of Belgium in the tournament's future organization:

- A great German player who deserves recognition for his outstanding play during the 1970's is RAINER BOSCH. In 1977 RAINER BOSCH and GERRY KINSELLA, in a sponsored wheelchair marathon, cover 1,000 kilometres from Hamburg in Germany to Liverpool, England in 13 days. Two days later in the final of a European invitation club tourament in Liverpool, while guesting for the Southport club, BOSCH scores twenty second-half points and steers Southport to victory.

DURING THE 1970's THE USA has some great players, particularly from the DETROIT SPARKS team:

- Comment has already been made of Bud Rumple and Denver Branum. The Sparks personified intimidation: GARY ODOROWSKI was the cool head of the team in the midst of Spark ignited frenzy, launching long range missiles into the basket and throwing countless blind passes through unsuspecting defenders; JOE SUTIKA, was a master defender as well as an adept passer and rebounder; DARRYL „TREE" WALLER, the swift titan who would become one of wheelchair basketball's most prolific scorers (see 1990's for profile); the Sparks' magician was MAURICE PHILLIPS, who along with David Kiley has authored some of the game's most brilliant passes, for example:
  As PHILLIPS once dashed towards his opponent's basket, his teammate WALLER launched a near full-court pass which fell short of its target. As PHILLIPS was quickly approaching the end-line, he suddenly extended both hands behi the-back of his chair and, much to everyon surprise, caught the ball. But the play did end with this great catch. PHILLIPS immedia threw a cross court behind-the-back pass w his left „hand" to a teammate who canned lay-up. Magic, sleight of hand – those are terms that come to mind when describing PH LIPS who, in addition to being an amputee of lower extremities, completed the aforement ned brilliant play with but two full fingers an thumb on his left hand and with only a compl thumb on his right!

Darryl „Tree" Waller and Baruch Hagai

IN 1977, AT THE FOURTH Men's European Champic ship in Raalte, the Netherlands, Israel enters Eu pean competition for the first time. Led by incomparable HAGAI and shooting guard MOS LEVI, they win gold ahead of the Netherlands a France. They repeat this performance in 1978 Lorient, France. France swaps places with Netherlands, winning the silver medal at this, fifth Men's European Championship.

Maurice Phillips, USA (left), Reggie Coltan (No. 42), Denver Branum (No. 44) and Willi Buchanan

THE DUTCH TEAM in the 197 and 1980's is coached ROB VERHEUVEL, who alo with Robert Perri is one Europe's top two coach over a twenty year peric The Dutch team by the l 1970's has some great pl ers amongst its ranks incl ding shooting guard/ ba handler HARRY VENEM FRITS STREYL, one of Eur pe's first big men and t ever improving FRITS WIE MANN. But the great play that makes the Dutch te tick is undoubtedly HE MAKKENZE:

Henk Makkenze's court control

HENK MAKKENZE – He was captain of the Dutch team from a very early age, a very shrewd move by coach Rob Verheuvel. Left-handed, he possessed a great twelve to fifteen-foot bank shot from either side of the court. He was the classic playmaker. He never turned his back to the action when he was in possession of the ball (a very necessary but rare skill amongst wheelchair basketball's top ballhandlers who frequently spin with the ball on a pick and roll and miss a passing opportunity to the weakside). Tactically very aware, he used this knowledge in defence to marshall the Dutch zone or „2-1-2" defences, revealing an unerring ability to know where the greatest threat would present itself. In order that he could play the game as he sensed it, he developed the principle of cambering the rear wheels of the chair and moving the axle forward of the rear upright. This gave him a far more manoeuvrable chair and a tremendous advantage over his opponents in the late 1970's. This, at a time when most players were still playing in refined versions of the E&J chair, which had first seen the light of day in the 1930's.

E SECOND WORLD CHAMPIONSHIP for Men takes place 1979 in Tampa, Florida. The USA confirms its sition as the top team in the world by defeating e Netherlands in the final, with France again winng bronze. Canada confirms its arrival into the p flight in Tampa by gaining fifth place with such and coming stars as REG MCCLELLAN at shoong guard, RON MINOR, a hustling guard and fast eak specialist, and highly talented forward TER COLISTRO.

E 1970's COMES TO A CLOSE with all players looking rward to the 1980 Paralympic Games in Arnhem, e Netherlands.

1980's – Wheelchair basketball opens its doors to amputee players and the new generation of wheelchairs captures the market

THE 1980 PARALYMPIC GAMES, originally scheduled for Moscow, are hosted by the Netherlands in Arnhem. Some of the US players arrive with the new „Quadra" box frame wheelchair which has the revolutionary quick release axle, making the chairs easier for storage in vehicles and thus ready for the mass market.

THIS IS THE FIRST TIME, in the men's tournament, since Tel Aviv in 1968, that the home nation has a realistic chance of victory. The Dutch team, superbly prepared by coach ROB VERHEUVEL is at its peak, with HENK MAKKENZE playing his greatest tournament. The USA squad fields several new faces, but DAVID KILEY is hellbent on his second successive Paralympic gold medal.

THE STAGE IS SET FOR the best men's Paralympic tournament yet seen. There excists a strong probability that the final would not occur between the USA and Israel for the first time since Tokyo in 1964. The semi-finals match up the Netherlands against the USA, who have defeated Israel by forty points in the pool match, and Israel against France. The French team, despite great play in the pool round to beat the Dutch, lack the cutting edge to get past Israel who progress to the final.

THE OTHER SEMI-FINAL is a classic game going down to the wire as the Netherlands defeats the USA 63 v 60 in front of 6,000 deliriously ecstatic home fans. This is the first time, in Arnhem, that wheelchair basketball players experience such spectator frenzy for their sport. PETER VAN VELSEN for the Netherlands is a major influence in his team's victory:

Peter van Velzen (No. 12), Coach Rob Verheuvel, Henk Makkenze (No. 6) and Harry Venema (from left), Arnhem 1980

- PETER VAN VELZEN – a great shooting small forward. In order for small forwards to play an inside game they have to be great exponents of the pick and roll and like the star small forward of the Israeli team, Joel Shafran, PETER was a master. He also possessed an excellent outside shot which was at its peak in Arnhem.

IN THE FINAL, THE WISE ISRAELIS exploit the fact that the Dutch had expended incredible amounts of energy on a very slow court, against the Americans in the semi-final. BARUCH HAGAI masterminds a low-scoring final, never allowing the Dutch stars to get into their stride. Israel wins their second Paralympic gold medal. Starring alongside HAGAI are MOSHE LEVI and JOEL SHAFRAN, a fast break and pick and roll genius.

Joel Shafran (left) and Curtis Bell

IN ARNHEM, AT THE WOMEN'S COMPETITION, Germany with new coach HELMUT ZDRENKA thrash Israel in the final 58 v 37. The USA wins its first Paralympic women's medal, the bronze.

IN 1981, THE SIXTH Men's European Championship takes place in Geneva and Israel retains the title, beating France in the final with the Netherlands winning bronze. France, though losing 74 v 68 in the final are on the verge of greatness. Two players who had helped the French B team beat Great Britain in the 1978 European Championship, MICHEL GRADELLE and ERIC BENAULT, are now coming of age. They play together in the Berck sur Mer club side in northern France and the one is the perfect foil for the other.

IT IS ANOTHER HIGHLY talented but volatile player for France, DOMINIQUE MARCHEGIANI, who is the key to France turning the tables on Israel in the final of the seventh Men's European Championship in Falun, Sweden in 1982.

Eric Benault (right), France and Raniero Bassi (playing for Switzerland)

France victory over Israel (63 v 58) signals the e of Israel's domination of European competiti during the late 1970's as well as its reign ov World and Paralympic competition, shared with t USA since 1968. Two factors cause the Israeli de line: a lack of new players and the team's difficul in adapting to the Player Classification System intr duced in 1984.

THIRD IN FALUN on home ground, is Sweden. Th performance signals the start of the purple peri for Swedish men's wheelchair basketball. Swed has possessed some great players since the ea 1970's such as LARS LÖVSTRÖM, ROLF JOHAN SON and INGVAR AGERMO. But it is only when fo mer swimming star LARS-GUNNAR ANDERSSO concentrates on wheelchair basketball, providi the forward power to complement Sweden's a time magical ballhandler and top scorer GUNNA BERGLUND that Sweden really begins to produ consistent performances. The Swedes would go o to win the gold medal at the 1982 Stoke Mandevi le Games.

- GUNNAR BERGLUND – the international whee chair basketball player with the most appeara ces at over 300. GUNNAR first played for Swede in the early 1970's and immediately hit th headlines with phenomenally accurate long distance shooting. Averaging ov twenty points a game througho his career, he could shoot from a distance and was at ease eith straight in the hoop or off the glas A tremendous wheelchair handl and ballhandler who could mesm rize defenders by daring to hold th ball in front of their faces. H extremely quick hands cause many turn overs by his opponent producing fast break baskets fo the quick guards of the Swedis team, Lars Lövström and Ro

Gunnar Berglund (left) and Frank Michael

Johansson. A great player who, at times, required better players around him to realize his true potential.

LUN PRODUCES ANOTHER historic moment in the devepment of the game. It is there one morning that HIL CRAVEN convinces STAN LABANOWICH of the eed for a fundamental change in the classification stem used in wheelchair basketball. LABANO'ICH, Chairman of the Basketball Section, the rerunner of the IWBF, decides to establish a playr classification committee under the Chairmanip of HORST STROHKENDL of Germany. The playr classification system is introduced at the 1984 aralympic Games in Stoke Mandeville.

OINCIDENTAL WITH DISCUSSIONS on the new classification system, the Stoke Mandeville authorities agree 1982 to allow players with other physical npairments, such as amputees, to play the game.

THE FIRST TIME THAT these additional players appear on the international scene is at the fourth Gold Cup (3rd World Championship) for men in Halifax, Nova Scotia, Canada in 1983. The USA, Canada, Sweden, the Netherlands, Israel and Great Britain take advantage of the inclusion of amputees in their teams.

THE TOURNAMENT IS a big disappointment for the rapidly improving Canadian team who, by losing in the last seconds to the French team in the pool round fail to qualify for the semi-finals. That loss results in a decline in the number of Canadian spectators. Canadian amputee players make their debut in Halifax are towering centre ROY SHERMAN, power forward FLO AUKEMA and future ball-handling maestro, PAT GRIFFIN. At guard is one of the world's best, if at times, inconsistent shooting guards MURRAY BROWN, who is partnered at that position by RICK HANSEN.

THE FRENCH QUALIFY to meet the USA in the final. It is the first time that CURTIS BELL of the USA had been allowed to partner his club teammate DAVID KILEY on the international stage. They are unstoppable, especially when consideration is given to some of the other members of the USA team: centre DARRYL WALLER; hustling guard DAVID EFFERSON; guard and co-playmaker with Kiley, RANDY SNOW; shooting guard, BOB MURDOCK and star defenders AL CAMPOS and JOE SUTIKA.

The US team celebrates victory: 5th Gold Cup, Melbourne, Australia 1986

The USA overwhelms France in the final 86 v 67 with Sweden winning an excellent bronze medal.

- CURTIS BELL – a player that can do it all: shoot, rebound and pass as well as play with great intelligence. Probably the greatest centre to have ever played the game. At 1.94 metres he is shorter than both Owen and Waller (each over 2.00 metres) but is a consummate athlete and one of the few players to have perfected wheelchair basketball's equivalent of the lean away „jump“ shot. On court, he had at times, an extra sensory

rapport with David Kiley. When the two players partnered each other in the US team, the USA never lost a match.
BELL won the MVP award at five NWBT's and was voted MVP at the 1986 Gold Cup in Melbourne, Australia. Definitely one of the world's greatest players.

AT THE 1984 PARALYMPIC GAMES in Stoke Mandeville, England, Germany continues to dominate women's wheelchair basketball with a third successful coach, CHRISTA BARTELS. LIESEL BRÖCKERHOFF becomes an important three-point shooting guard combining with shooting superstar HEIDI KIRSTE and all-round player JUTTA SAGGAU to beat Israel in the final 42 v 32. Japan wins the bronze medal for the first time.

IN THE MEN'S COMPETITION, the USA, having come to the tournament without BELL and KILEY defeat Canada in the quarter-finals, but once again meet the Dutch team in the semi-final and are beaten. The superior all-round team work and skills of the Dutch team are too much for the Americans, whose team play is based around twin towers DARRYL WALLER and ED OWEN.

Curtis Bell

FRANCE, HAVING BEATEN Sweden in the other semi-final, goes on to record a memorable victory over the Netherlands 68 v 61 in the final to win their first Paralympic gold medal. The Dutch have again suffered from a titanic semi-final battle with the USA but the French team, captained by shooting guard MARC GUILLEMAIN, are magnificent. Other French players winning gold at Stoke Mandeville are ANDRÉ CHAUVE, a great ballhandler and conduit for discussion between the players and the coach, ROBERT PERRI; MAURICE CLAEYS an excellent passer and redoubtable defender; shooting guard MICHEL IZANIC; CELESTIN PARSEMAIN, a great rebounder and clever forward; ALAIN TROLONG, a mercurial point guard with an outstanding left-handed outside shot and DOMINIQUE MARCHEGIANI. Above all, the two players who make the difference over the excellent Dutch team are MICHEL GRADELLE and ERIC BENAULT:

■ MICHEL GRADELLE – a player who at the age of seventeen was somewhat uncoordinated, he became the best wheelchair handler in the world. He possessed blistering acceleration, which he would use to great effect to blow by both suspecting and unsuspecting defenders. He would send defenders the wrong way with the slightest dip of the head or shoulders, with or without the ball. Expert at the pick and roll, he always had the option to pass inside to the forward, or sink an outside shot from any distance. His change of pace and direction gave him countless possibilities to penetrate the key to score scoop shots, hook shots and straight forward lay-ups. His speed of movement intimidated all but the most able adversaries. He was renowned for making unbelievable interceptions, then streaking away to score simple lay-ups. In the 1990 Gold Cup against the USA, he scored repeated outside shots from the left side when penetration to the basket was blocked by the aggressive US zone defence. One of the greatest ball-handling magicians the game has ever seen and a perfect, if at times, highly strung partner to the sang froid of his club teammate Eric Benault.

■ ERIC BENAULT – French centre from 1979 to 1992 and captain towards the end of his career. ERIC was the equal of Curtis Bell as a centre. Bell's athleticism might have made him a greater all-round player. At nearly two metres, Eric Benault was the first European player who could rival the giant American threesome of Bell, Owen and Waller. He had perfect technique when setting a pick for Gradelle to take the roll. In defence, he mastered blocking out prior to turning in for the rebound. A great calming influence on the French team if one of its more exuberant members lost his cool. He retired from internationa competition at the relatively young age of 34.

IN THE FIGHT FOR THE bronze medal, Sweden com back from the dead to beat the USA.

AFTER THE MEN'S FINAL in Stoke Mandeville, Dutc coach Rob Verheuvel, makes a significant quot

Michel Gradelle

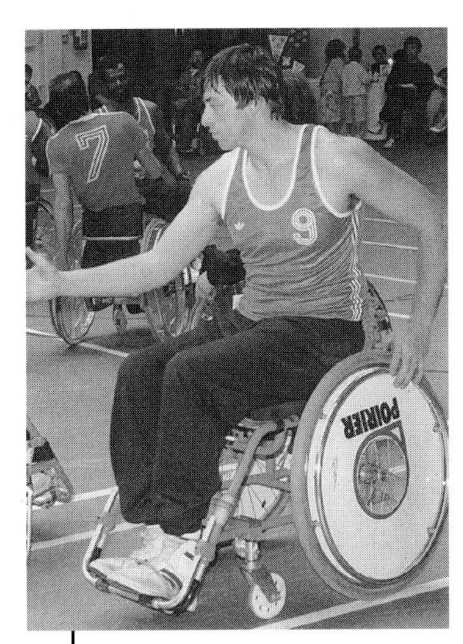

Eric Benault

›ncerning the newly introduced player classifica-
on sytem: „I was concerned that the new classifi-
ation sytem, by ensuring a place on court for the
ss physically mobile players, would reduce the
andard of play in international wheelchair bas-
etball. This final has proved my concerns to be
nfounded".

1985 AND 1986, the men's tournament at Stoke
andeville reverts to a single division. The top
ams in the world concentrate on the Gold Cup,
e European Championship and the Paralympic
ames. This permits teams in the second level to
rogress. In 1985, Spain beats Great Britain for the
old medal with Australia placing third.

HE EMERGENCE OF SPAIN on the world scene is clear-
related to the development of one of the game's
reatest shooters and rebounders, ANTONIO HEN-
RES, who had started playing for the Spanish team
1975 in the era of JOSE SABATE JAURES and LUIS
LBELDA BERRAL.

IN AUSTRALIA, DAVID GOULD, a future superstar starts to play the game in 1982 which coincides with the retirement of some of the Australian players from the early days such as KEVIN COOMBS. Considerable investment by the Australians in the 1980's and 1990's, will ensure their movement up the world rankings in both men's and women's wheelchair basketball by the mid 1990's.

GREAT BRITAIN, IN 1985/1986, owes its reemergence onto the world scene to the coaching of MICHAEL MCCREADIE and the development of a pool of highly talented young players, assisted by the lingering influence of one or two old-timers.

THE FOURTH WORLD CHAMPIONSHIP for Men (fifth Gold Cup) takes place in Melbourne, Australia in 1986. The USA, KILEY and BELL, beat Canada in the final. The Netherlands defeat France and its temperamental superstar MICHEL GRADELLE for the bronze medal. The Canadians for the first time realize their true potential, with REG MCCLELLAN controlling both the Canadian offence and defence to great effect:

- REG MCCLELLAN – An outstanding two-point playmaker who never missed a chance to get the ball to the big men inside. As a shooter he probably did not reach his full potential, owing to his belief in always passing to the player with the best opportunity to score. A great team man and captain who constantly fought for the Canadians to believe in their own ability. He achieved this goal at the Melbourne Gold Cup.

IN THE POOL MATCHES in Melbourne, an epic match takes place between the Netherlands and Israel. Wheelchair basketball fans see the last "head to head" confrontation between BARUCH HAGAI and HENK MAKKENZE. The match goes down to the wire with the Netherlands and MAKKENZE winning in the last few seconds.

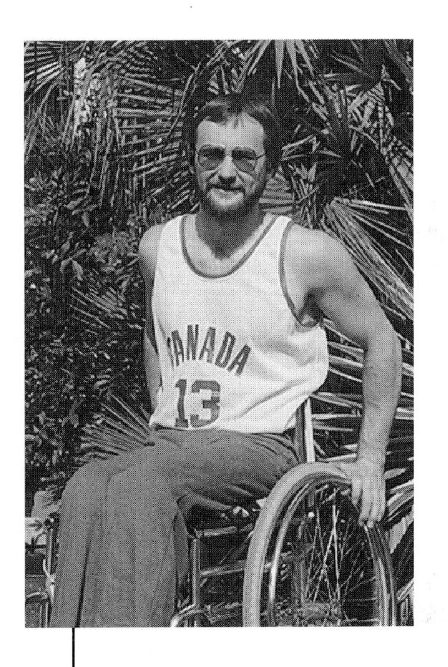

Reg McClellan

ANOTHER PERFORMANCE of note in the pool matches in Melbourne, is the clash between the USA and Yugoslavia. The Yugoslavs (future Slovenians) send shock waves through the American camp by holding a first-half lead, but the USA comes back to win in the second half. Yugoslavia is led by power shooting forward IGOR DUBROVSKI, who is ably supported by small forward LAZO LJUBOTINA and shooting guard MARIAN TRDINA.

THE EIGHTH MEN'S EUROPEAN CHAMPIONSHIP takes place in Lorient, France in 1987. France confirms its hold on the title by defeating the Dutch in the final. Belgium comes from nowhere to win the bronze medal. This is probably their finest performance in the modern era. MARC DEVOS is outstanding at shooting guard.

LORIENT, FRANCE IN 1987 also sees the second Women's European Championship. Germany again beats Israel in the final, but the bronze medal is won by the Netherlands. This is the first sign of a change in the balance of power in European women's wheelchair basketball.

DURING THE 1980's, several excellent women are making great strides in their countries to get more women and girls to play the game. Of particular note are HELEN RÖNNGARD of Sweden, SUE HOBBS from Australia and ELAINE ELL, DIANE EARL and DIANE HRYCHUK (née PIDSKALNY) of Canada.

TOWARDS THE END OF THE 1980's, major wheelchair basketball tournaments are coming thick and fast for both men and women. In October 1988 the world's best teams come together in Seoul, South Korea for the Men's and Women's Paralympic Finals.

FOR THE FIRST TIME, the USA brings a women's team that possesses a realistic chance of winning gold at the Paralympic finals:

- The USA's women had taken wheelchair basketball more seriously following the establishment of the first national Women's Wheelchair Basketball Tournament (NWWBT)in 1976. In 1976 and 1977, the NWWBT was won by the Canadian national team; therefore, the NWWBT permitted two countries to become serious about the game. In later years, that tournament motivated Mexico to initiate a programme for women. Women were now organizing their own tournaments, rather than letting the men pay lip service to their efforts.

THE US SQUAD IN SEOUL IS led on offence, by DEBORAH SUNDERMAN, who dominates the boards at both ends of the court and is top scorer. The US defence is outstanding and unsettles the Germans. The US hustling guards make the difference, particularly are SHARON HEDRICK, SUSAN HAGEL and SHERRY RAMSEY.

Deborah Sundermann (left)

The USA beats Germany in the final 38 v 31: that brings to an end the German dynasty which had endured for twelve years. The Netherlands continues to show improving form and wins the bronze medal.

Sharon Hedrick and Bob Szyman

IN THE MEN'S COMPETITION, the USA has organized a extremely strong squad. KILEY and BELL star i tandem along with ED OWEN, appearing in his la Paralympic Games. The Americans also have son young blood in the team. In particular, MIK SCHLAPPI competes his first Paralympic Games. H will develop, in the 1990's, into one of the greate 1.5-point players the world has ever seen.

Mike Schlappi (No. 3) and Darren Schenebeck (No. 4)

German men's team in 1988

IE USA DEFEATS THE Netherlands in the final 74 v 63. ance overcomes Germany for the bronze. It is the st tournament for those great adversaries, HENK AKKENZE and BARUCH HAGAI. However, the therlands has found MAKKENZE's replacement in agical playmaker GERT-JAN VAN DER LINDEN, 10 will lead them into the 1990's. At centre, e Netherlands possesses a trump card in EN KLERKS, who ving started his reer at the 984 Paralympic imes, has now atured into a eat player rival- g Benault and ll in his effec- eness under the ards.

Norbert Weinrauter

1989, THE NTH Men's Euro- ean Champions- p and the third omen's Europe- Championship kes place in Charleville-Mezière, France. In the en's competition, France retains the title it had st won at the 1982 championship. The Nether- nds again takes the silver and the rapidly impro- ng Germans capture the bronze.

Special mention must be made here of some tremendous German players during the 1980's who, with the assistance of coach ULF MEHRENS, fought their way up the international rankings to become major forces in the early 1990's. NORBERT WEINRAUTER, an ex-professional boxer was Germany's all-time top scorer, achieving this great record with a two-handed shot owing to weakened wrists incurred during an accident; BERTL SCHAUBERGER, a point guard and hustling defender; FRANK MICHAEL,

Frank Michael

Germany's first really effective forward; HOLGER GLINICKI, a very tough one-point shooting guard; WOLFGANG SCHÄFER, multi purpose forward or guard who could have had a more illustrious career if his studies had not intervened; and PAUL KÜHNREICH, a deadly shooting guard.

THINGS AGAIN DO NOT GO as planned for the German women's team. They are beaten in the final by a rapidly improving Dutch side with MAAIKE SMIT and INGE TIGGELMANN giving great support to power forward ADA KOK.

THE FINAL TOURNAMENT of the 1980's is staged at the Stoke Mandeville Games, where Canada thrash a very strong USA team 68 v 50. The USA team includes DAVID KILEY and future superstars REGGIE COLTON and TROOPER JOHNSON. REG MCCLELLAN again weaves his magic at point/shooting guard and is ably assisted by new shooting guard and one point-wonder, MICHAEL FROGLEY, who could

USA - Canada at Stoke Mandeville in 1987: Reg McClellan, Bruce Russel, David Kiley (No. 12), Reggie Coltan, Mike Frogley (No. 6), Jim Enright, Trooper Johnson (No. 14) and Darren Schenebeck (No.4) (from left)

knock down perimeter shots with either hand. ROY HENDERSON is a key player in the Canadian team being able to play at forward, despite being a two-point player. Other key players in the Canadian team are BRUCE RUSSELL at forward, point guard

PAT GRIFFIN, as well as shock troop, fast break specialist and ball handler DENIS LAPALME and small forward JIM ENRIGHT, who has developed into the world's most effective exponent of setting the pick on a pick and roll. ENRIGHT is also a superb defender.

ONE OF THE DISAPPOINTMENTS of the 1970's and 1980's was the continuing absence of the Italian men's team as a major force. Special mention must be made of two Italian players: CARLO DI GIUSTO, one of Europe's top power forwards and CARLO IANNUCCI, an outstanding shooting guard.

THE LATE1980's sees the retirement of some of the greatest players the world has ever seen, but there are many willing and eager future heroes waiting in the wings to fill their places.

1990's – 1st Women's Gold Cup and expansion on all continents

FOR THE FIRST TIME, in 1990, women's and men's world championships take place: The women play in St. Etienne, France. The final between the USA and Germany is one of the greatest games ever seen, with the USA finally taking gold 58 v 55. Deborah Sunderman again stars for the USA but special mention has to be made of tremendous performances by the two greatest 1.5-point players in the game during the 1980's and 1990's, SUSAN HAGEL of the USA and HEIDI KIRSTE of Germany:

- SUSAN HAGEL – the powerhouse of the US team who will fight down to the last breath for her country. A great shooter who can come up with the big baskets at the right moment, the sign of a great player. In defence SUSAN has that vital ability that coaches seek, in that when confronted by a four-point power forward she will not envisage any mismatch and will, therefore, defend well beyond her classification pointage thus giving a vital boost to the team.

Susan Hagel

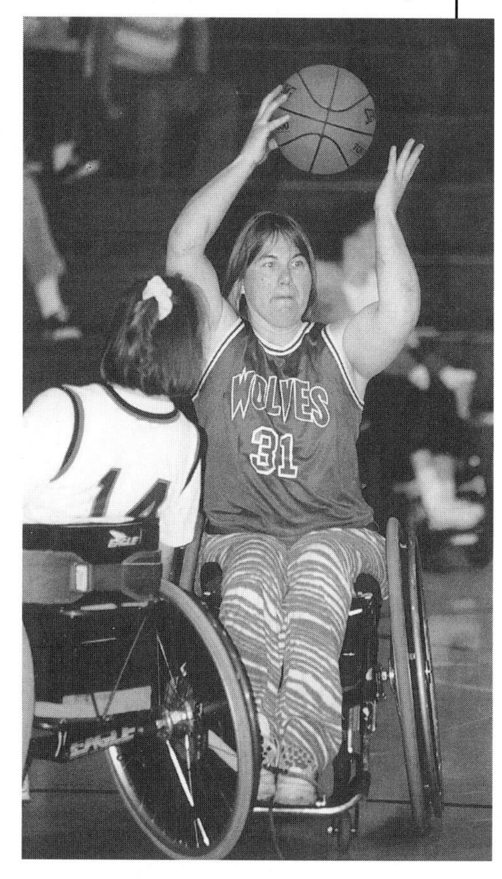

- HEIDI KIRSTE – a high scoring shooting guard who scored 23 points in the 1990 Gold Cup final including a three-pointer. An aggressive defender who is probably shaded by Susan Hagel in this part of her game, but as a shooter she is in a class of her own.

CANADA WINS the bronze medal in St. Etienne, signalling its arrival amongst the world's top women's wheelchair basketball nations.

FOR THE MEN, the fifth World Championship and sixth Gold Cup comes back to its roots in Bruges, Belgium in early August 1990. The USA has a powerful team including DAVID KILEY and titan, DARRYL WALLER. They come up against a French team th is at the zenith of its abillty under new coach, MA RICE SCHOENACKER. In the final, two of the worl great centres ERIC BENAULT and DARRYL WALL cancel each other out under the boards. It is t French guard quartet led by the mercurial MICH GRADELLE, and including JEAN YVES REGNAU PHILIPPE NUTTIN and LIONEL CHAVANNE, w pass the ball around the key repeatedly finding t open man, normally GRADELLE, for the fifteen fo shot. Early in the second half, the French have seventeen-point lead but the USA is not finish and, with KILEY showing some flashes of brillianc claws the lead back to one point. KILEY's efforts a bolstered by teammate ALBERT CAMPOS who n

Heidi Kirste

only plays his customarily brilliant defence, b scores many key baskets as well. In the last secon the USA has the chance to snatch victory from t jaws of defeat, but the French hang on to record a historic victory 62 v 61. In the bronze medal gam Canada defeats a disappointing Dutch team. Austr lia beats Germany for fifth place, thereby recordi

French team at Bruges in 1990

THE USA ARE NARROW favourites to win both gold medals, though many countries, in the warm-up matches prior to the Games, have shown they are ready to take on the best in both tournaments. The pool matches produce some fine encounters. In the men's quarter-final, Germany beats the fancied British team and then loses to the Netherlands in the semi-final. In the other semi-final, the USA takes its revenge on France for their 1990 Gold Cup defeat, setting up a repeat of the 1988 Men's Paralympic final. In a very low scoring match, the USA beats the Netherlands 39 v 36 and is awarded the gold medal.

USA v The Netherlands at Bruges in 1990: (from left) Servaas Kamerling (No. 12), David Efferson (No. 13), Ben Klerks (No. 15), Darryl „Tree" Waller (No. 15), Gert-Jan van der Linden (No. 10), Darren Schenebeck (No. 4)

s highest ever position in World or Paralympic ompetition.

1991, THE TENTH Men's European Championship nd the fourth Women's European Championship ke place in Ferrol, Spain. France again defeats the etherlands 57 v 50 in the final. A re-emergent am from Great Britain wins the bronze against rael 85 v 59.

THE WOMEN'S CHAMPIONSHIP, a great battle is waged the final between Germany and the Netherlands. e lead constantly switches throughout the second half and Germany ultimately wins in overtime, 49 v 48. Corinna Robitschko records her final victory over the Netherlands led by superstar MARJA LEEUWEN LOKKER.

IN BARCELONA in August 1992, wheelchair basketball grabs the headlines attracting 12,500 spectators to many of the men's and women's Paralympic matches played in the historic Badalona arena.

FOR THE AMERICANS, BELL and KILEY play in their final Paralympic Games, but the final is won by inspired performances from the newcomers to the USA team, led by TIM KAZEE, REGGIE COLTON and MIKE SCHLAPPI.

IT IS THE FINAL MATCH for the Dutch superstar duo of shooting guard FRITS WIEGMANN and BEN KLERKS:

- FRITS WIEGMANN – one of the greatest shooters the world has ever seen using a two-handed set shot, frequently launched from behind Ben Klerks's screen. He was the classic case of a player who loves the game and maximizes his potential. He had to use a two-handed shot owing to polio having affected his upper, as well as his lower limbs. In club competition, he would regularly score thirty or even forty points per match. If a defender came out to check the shot he would send a hook pass inside to Ben Klerks, who would have rolled off the screen to can the lay-up.

The Netherlands men's team at Assen in 1990

Frits Wiegmann (right) and Coach Rob Verheuvel, Arnhem 1980

- BEN KLERKS – a dominating centre or power forward who brought a world class dimension to the Dutch team in these positions. Frequently teaming up with Frits Wiegmann to provide a solid screen from behind which Frits could bury both shots and opponents. He also combined well with the the young bucks and unsung heroes on the Dutch side, SERVAAS KAMERLING and RENE MARTENS, with whom he perfected the rap-around play on the right side which gave him a drive along the baseline to the basket. BEN in the latter part of his career, developed an excellent bank shot from the right when his path to the basket for the lay-up was blocked.

IN THE BRONZE MEDAL GAME, Germany pulls off a surprise defeat of the French, a result which heralds declining fortunes for the once great French team.

FOLLOWING THE FINAL, a positive test for the use of a painkiller by David Kiley leads to the USA's disqualification. The medals are redistributed and the Netherlands, for the first time ever, gains the gold medal.

Ben Klerks

THE WOMEN PRODUCE the first great Paralympic tou nament. Newcomer, Australia, forces its way in the semi-final which relegates Germany to fight fo at best, fifth place. In the final, based on their po match performances, the USA starts as favourit and sets up an aggressive expanded zone defen with the hope of containing the highly talented Canadians, coached by TIM FRICK. The Canadians have other ideas and possess a superstar in CHANTAL BENOIT who explodes onto the Paralympic scene in front of 12,500 spectators and rips the USA's defence to ribbons. Out of a final score of 35 points for Canada and 26 for the USA, CHANTAL nets eighteen with eight field goals and two free shots.

THE NETHERLANDS, in the bronze medal match, are too strong for Australia defeating them 42 v 33.

Chantal Benoit

1993, THE ELEVENTH Men's European Championship and fifth Women's European Championship take place in Berlin.

IN THE WOMEN'S COMPETITION, the Netherlands clearly confirm its standing as the top team in Europe by defeating Germany 53 v 38 in the final.

Marja van Leeuwen Lokker (No. 11)

- MARJA LEEUWEN LOKKER – One of the most outstanding shooting forwards to ever play the women's game. She learnt her trade in Dutch men's competition. A fearless competitor, LOKKER possesses an excellent outside shot and a rare ability to penetrate the key with great regularity. In defence, she takes the centre of the key in a „2-1-2" formation which she controls with great ability. MARJA is undoubtedly one of the greatest players in the world but requires greater talent around her in the Dutch team for her to lead the Netherlands to Paralympic or World Championship gold.

FRANCE REPEATS its performance from Ferrol in 1991 and wins the bronze medal.

IN THE MEN'S COMPETITION Great Britain, who won bronze in Ferrol, continue to improve and confront the Netherlands in the final. A virtuoso performance by GERT-JAN VAN DER LINDEN in the first half, who scores repeatedly from the perimeter at two and three-point range, give the Dutch an eighteen point lead early in the second half. VAN DER LINDEN's performance is ably supported by Dutch hustling guards SERVAAS KAMERLING, RENE MARTENS and ANTON DE ROOY who underline time and time again the need for highly mobile guards in any successful international team of the 1990's. SANDER MARKUS also plays an important roll at small forward.

GREAT BRITAIN FIGHT their way back into the match, tying the score with two and a half minutes left on the clock. Great Britain fall into foul trouble and in pushing aggressively for victory put new Dutch shooting forward KOEN JANSENS to the line on six occasions. He scores five of the free shots and gives the Dutch a five-point victory 57 v 52. This is the first time the Netherlands has won the title.

- GERT-JAN VAN DER LINDEN – The world's greatest point guard of the 1990's, accumulating the following record as a result of his gold medal performance at the 1992 Paralympic Games in Barcelona: tournament joint highest percentage free throw shooter at 71%, tournament highest 3-point scorer, tournament first in steals, tournament first in assists. GERT-JAN has been in love with the sport of wheelchair basketball since childhood and has immersed himself in the sport since that time. He tests the rules to the limit but always in a positive way and demonstrates great respect for other players' abilities. In European Champions Cup competition, he has been in the winning side eight times since

Gert-Jan van der Linden (left)

1984 and second or third on the other four occasions. He has earned five MVP awards. His record speaks for itself. He has been Europe's number one point guard for a ten year period, rivalling David Kiley as the world's number one over the same period, until that player's retirement. His ability intimidates all but the most competent opponents.

- SERVAAS KAMERLING – The human dynamo of the Dutch team. He epistomises the hustling guard who never gives the opposing ball handler a second's respite. He has been an outstanding player since his debut in the Dutch youth team in the early 1980's. While playing for the youth team at Stoke Mandeville, he was once observed playing throughout a tournament with serious tissue damage to his back, all in the cause of his team. Great chair control made him a consummate defender and a great setter of the pick for his teammates to take the roll. Dedication paid resulting in the gradual development of an excellent around perimeter shot and he was always a threat on the fast break.

FRANCE DEFEATED GERMANY for the bronze medal and the Spanish men's team signalled their continuing improvement.

PRIOR TO THE 1994 Gold Cup for Men the IWBF, for the first time, organizes qualification tournaments in Rio de Janeiro, Brazil and Tehran, I.R.Iran. Japan defeats Australia in Tehran and the world is introduced to a potentially great one-point player in HIROSHI IWANO. In Rio de Janeiro, the USA is too strong for its South American rivals and qualifies, under new coach, BRAD HEDRICK, for the Gold Cup finals along with Argentina and Brazil. Coincidental with the Rio de Janeiro qualification tournament is the first South American Nations Championship which is won by Argentina with Brazil capturing second, Uruguay third and Venezuela fourth.

Servaas Kamerling

Hiroshi Iwano

THE SEVENTH GOLD CUP for Men (sixth World Cha pionship) takes place in Edmonton, Alberta, Ca da in July 1994. Never have so many teams com ted capable of playing top flight wheelchair bask ball in one tournament. Demonstrating the inc dible standards characterizing this tournament capable German team struggles to finish nin Talented Spain beats Sweden for the seventh po tion. The Netherlands (the reigning Paralympic a European champions) defeat Australia by th points for the fifth position.

IN THE FIRST SEMI-FINAL, the USA crushes Canada 8 50. Great Britain then comes back from the de against France in the second semi-final. After tr ling by five points with 23 seconds remaining the clock:

- JOE JAYARATNE scores a long three-pointer w 15 seconds left. Then SIMON MUNN interce the inbounded pass. As he shoots, an intentio foul is called against the French. MUNN th scores one of the two shots leaving Great Brit only one point behind with three seconds and with possession of the ball at the half-w line. STEVE CAINE inbounds to DAN JOHNS on the left-hand side of the key who drains shot as the buzzer sounds. Great Britain clai a spot in the final against the USA.

'HE FINAL, Great Britain, who were twelfth and last he 1990 Gold Cup, take on the might of the USA. he half, the USA has a four-point lead 30 v 26. score remains close until the last five minutes

Steve Caine

en the USA pulls away to a 67 v 53 victory. The team has a tremendous starting five made up of)OPER JOHNSON, MIKE SCHLAPPI and MARK EPHERD at shooting guard, REGGIE COLTON at ward and DARRYL WALLER at centre. This five is well balanced that they all score ten or more nts, with SCHLAPPI, SHEPHERD and COLTON h recording fourteen. The Great Britain squad duces a true team performance throughout the rnament, but lacks the fire power of the Ameri- first five players. Key players in the GB team in final are point guards COLIN PRICE and STEVE NE, shooting guards JOE JAYARATNE, MARK EANEY and DAN JOHNSON, forwards CALUM RDON, DAVE BRAMLEY and TONY WOOLLARD at centre SIMON MUNN.

■ REGGIE COLTON – At the banquet after the final in Edmonton, REGGIE was voted unanimously MVP for the seventh Gold Cup. There had been tremendous improvements in COLTON's all-

Reggie Colton

round play in the two years since Barcelona. In particular his shooting action from the free throw line was a revelation. A tremendous foil to Darryl „Tree" Waller, the USA's first five possessed all the options with COLTON and Waller inside and with the three shooting guards around the perimeter if the inside shot was not available. Already a great player with further potential for improvement, COLTON is most of all, a gentleman on court.

■ DARRYL WALLER – In his later years, developed a more all-round game, similar to the great Ed Owen. With new US coach Brad Hedrick, WALLER is a great practitioner of the back pick in the defensive half of the court in order to gain a man advantage on attack. Definitely, one of the world's top five centres along with Curtis Bell, Eric Benault, Ben Klerks and Ed Owen.

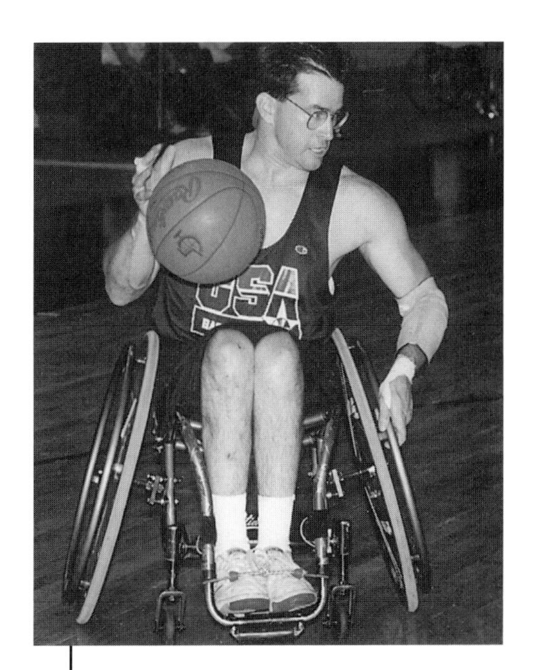

Mike Schlappi

■ MIKE SCHLAPPI – a tremendous 1.5-point hustling guard who has great mobility, using it effectively to press the ballhandler and still recover if a pick is set against him. Like Waller, he is a great exponent of the back pick which is one of the corner stones of Brad Hedrick's coaching manual. One of the world's great class one players and a member of the all-star team at the 1994 Gold Cup.

JOINING COLTON AND SCHLAPPI on the all-star team at the awards banquet in Edmonton are MARK CHEANEY of Great Britain, DAVID GOULD of Australia, KOEN JANSENS of the Netherlands and PHILIPPE NUTTIN of France.

Ann Wild

IN AUGUST 1994, the second Women's Gold Cup takes place at Stoke Mandeville, England, with the big four (Canada, USA, the Netherlands and Australia) from Barcelona vying for the medals.

THE POOL MATCHES go to form. Canada and Australia qualify for the semi-finals from Pool A and the USA as well as the Netherlands from Pool B. The pool matches between the top two in each pool are titanic struggles, a sign that intense competition will dominate the semi-finals and the medal finals.

IN THE CROSS-OVER MATCHES for the classification of the fifth through eighth places, Great Britain, led by ANN WILD, pulls off a surprise victory (38 v 37) against Japan, who have tournament top scorer and rebounder CHIKA UEMURA. Germany defeats Great Britain for fifth place.

IN THE SEMI-FINALS, Canada defeats the Netherlands 39 v 31 and the USA beats Australia 33 v 29. Like the Men's Gold Cup two weeks earlier, the women produce many close and exciting matches which have the English wheelchair basketball fans' entranced.

IN THE BRONZE MEDAL MATCH, MARJA LEEUWEN LOKKER scores 22 points and grabs 11 rebounds to help her team close a second half deficit of 11 points. Then LOKKER ties the score with 55 seconds left on the clock. With 13 seconds left, AMANDA ROSE scores the basket she will remember all her life and wins the bronze for Australia 38 v 36. Australia receives other great performances from power forward LIESL TESCH, forward SHARON SLANN and shooting guards LISA O'NION and DONNA RITCHIE. For the Netherlands, MAAIKE SMIT gives great support to LOKKER.

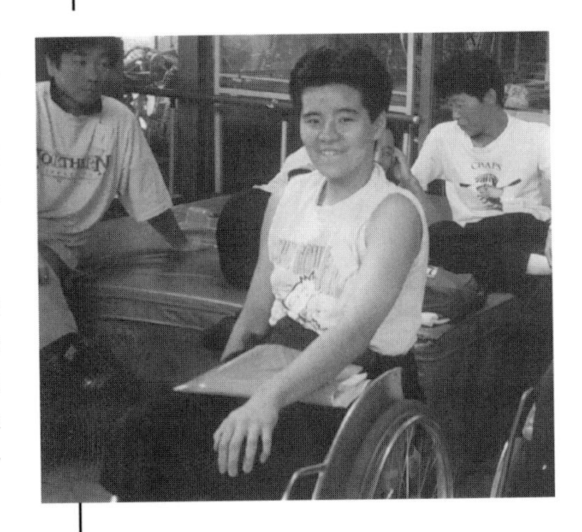

Chika Uemura

IN THE FINAL, CANADA, by half time, has built up a 13 point lead. Although this lead is reduced to 8 points early in the second half, the Americans are kept at bay by the scoring of CHANTAL BENOIT and RENÉE LEDREW. Canada wins the final 45 v 34 and are confirmed as the best team in the world. For Canada, RENÉE LEDREW, at her first international tournament produces some outstanding performance at power forward, LINDA KUTROWSKI plays another captain's role at point guard and is ably assisted by up and coming TRACEY FERGUSON. However, it is Canada's superstar from Barcelona, CHANTAL BENOIT, who comes through when it matters and assures the Canadian victory by scoring 1[illegible] points.

■ CHANTAL BENOIT – may not be very tall, but i[illegible] a powerhouse all purpose guard who play[illegible] great defence and moves rapidly in transitio[illegible]

Australian women's team at 1st Gold Cup, St. Etinne 1990: (from left) Coralie Crucheti, Julie Russel, Sharon Slann, Mandy Rose, Amanda Carter, Lisa O'Nion, Donna Ritchie (standing from left) Kaylene Kranz (Manager), Sue Hobbs, Peter Corr (Coach), Paula Ewin, Linda Ross (Nurse) and Liesl Tesch

onto the fast break. She is a good shooter from outside but excels at penetrating the key when all other options are sewn up by the opposing team. A great player, BENOIT was the key to Canada's gold medal performances in both Barcelona 1992 and Stoke Mandeville 1994.

Canadian women's team at Stoke Mandevilee in 1994

FOR THE USA, SUSAN HAGEL scores 10 points, demonstrating the importance of having an oustanding class one player if any team wishes to be successful at the international level. New players for the USA who will go on to impress in the late 1990's are JAMIE DANSKIN WITHLOW and RUTH NUNEZ who, at the banquet that evening, is awarded the tournament MVP.

THAT SAME EVENING LIESL TESCH of Australla, RENÉE LEDREW and LINDA KUTROWSKI of Canada, MAAIKE SMIT of the Netherlands and one-point guard from Japan, JUNKO SAKOU are honoured as all-stars. Women's wheelchair basketball has really arrived on the world scene.

Renée Ledrew

JULY, 1995 SEES the twelfth Men's European Championship in Paris, France. The pool-round matches are full of surprises. Austria defeats Germany for the first time, and by 25 points! This victory is a fitting tribute to one of the game's great unsung heroes, Austrian playmaker and shooting guard, WALTER PFALLER, who for fifteen years has been a tower of strength for his country. The Finns overcome Sweden by a similar margin. If Italy had not squandered a twelve point lead to the Finns in the last three minutes of their pool match, they would have moved through to the semi-finals, depriving France of a semi-final place for the first time in the history of the European Championships. Italy's young team, led by veteran power forward CARLO DI GIUSTO, had beaten France in an earlier pool match. Italy finish ninth in the tournament!

IN THE TOP OF POOL A MATCH, Spain wins a thrilling overtime victory, 78 v 77 against the Netherlands. The two top teams in pool B, Great Britain and France, are also involved in an overtime duel with Great Britain winning 61 v 59, after NIGEL SMITH's winning three-pointer passes through the net as the buzzer sounds at the end of the five minute overtime period.

THE TOP FIVE TEAMS from this competition qualify for the Atlanta Paralympic Games giving great importance to the 5th and 6th place play-off match between Germany and Sweden. The Germans, having arrived in Paris hopeful of a medal, are beaten by the Swedes 68 v 57 with GUNNAR BERGLUND still weaving his magic.

THE SEMI-FINALS MATCH France against Spain and the Netherlands against Great Britain: The Spain versus France match is an epic long-range shooting battle between the two great shooting forwards from Spain, ANTONIO HENARES and DIEGO DE PAZ, and PHILIPPE BAYE's French squad. Spain win this thriller, again in overtime, 69 v 64.

Walter Pfaller

- ANTONIO HENARES – Possibly the greatest shooting forward the men's game has ever seen, repeatedly establishing himself as top scorer in Paralympic and Gold Cup Tournaments. In Barcelona at the 1992 Paralympic Games finals, ANTONIO was tournament top scorer with 24.88 points per game, tournament highest free-throw shooter, tournament top percentage 3-point shooter and tournament top rebounder with 13.25 per game. At the 1994 Gold Cup in Edmonton, he topped all scorers, scoring 23.3 points and averaging 10 rebounds per game. Why is he the best shooter in the world? He has cultivated a perfect shooting action which possesses great strength, great control, a high release and a perfect follow-through. As he comes to the end of his career, he is schooling

Antonio Henares

his heir apparent DIEGO DE PAZ who, in Edmonton, was the tournament's highest rebounder with 12.1 rebounds per game while scoring 15 points per game. Another great skill practised by Antonio, who is not the tallest rebounder in the world, is blocking out on the shot before turning in for the rebound. In his career, to date, ANTONIO has won 25 MVP's in international and international club competition.

THE NETHERLANDS and Great Britain start cautiously in their semi-final, but Great Britain establishes a half-time lead. The Dutch come out in the second half and threaten to blow the British away scoring 18 points without reply. Enter centre stage, MARK CHEANEY, the greatest one-point shooter the world has ever seen, to score 22 points and win the day for Great Britain, 56 v 52.

- MARK CHEANEY – Like most one-point players, it has taken him many years to perfect his allround game. Extremely quick hands permit him to protect the ball while, at the same time, taunting the best power forwards in the world with the idea that they might be able take the ball away from him.
  His shooting skills are incredible, having perfected a classic release of the ball while maintaining trunk stability, a technique that is rarely mastered by one point players. Redoubtable in defence, he has developed many defensive plays

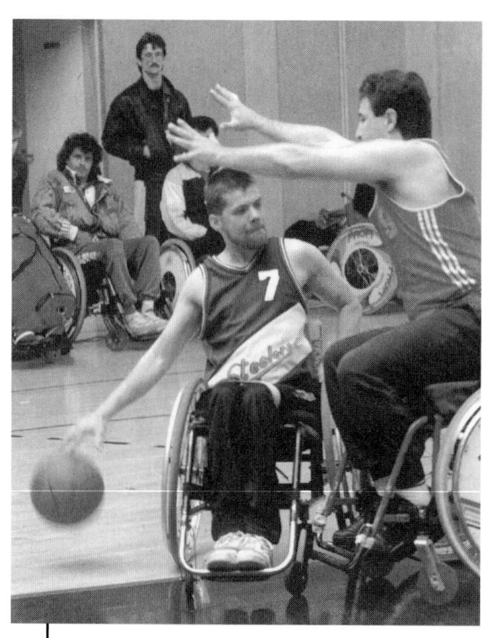

Mark Cheaney

over time to stop the most mobile of opponen
A one-point player who scores 20 points p
match at the international level, particula
when defences know of his capabilities, has ea
ned the highest respect. He is an expert at ho
ding position on court, always being ready
receive the assist and possessing a quick, hi
release on the shot. These are the keys
MARK's success.

Colin Price, GB, (right) and Carlo di Giusto, Italy

- COLIN PRICE – a winner through and throug
who over ten years has developed into one of th
world's most dynamic shooting/point guard
Extremely aggressive in defence, COLIN can tur
defeat into victory through his own determina
tion, incredible reserves of energy and electr
skills. A man devoted to the team's success, h
took time to realize that the best way to assu
victory for his team was to carry his teammat
with him when sounding the charge for victor

By continual improvement in this area, he could become one of the game's few complete players. An outstanding shooter, who in the warm-up, would frequently belie his shooting potential, but once into the match could string together four, six or even eight successive baskets. His points come from fast break baskets, from driving through the key for spinning lay-ups or by shooting the eye of the ring from mid distance.

THE NETHERLANDS BEAT the French convincingly for the bronze medal 64 v 45 and this sets up, for the first time ever, a European Championship final between Spain and Great Britain.

GREAT BRITAIN STRUGGLES to overcome Spain's lead through most of the match. Midway through the second half, DIEGO DE PAZ threatens to take the match beyond Great Britain scoring two consecutive, towering, three-pointers. With the Spanish holding a six-point lead, STEVE CAINE turns the game around, scoring two three-pointers which combined with ANTONIO HENARES's departure for his fifth foul, help Great Britain win a tense final, 55 v 54. The British team wins its first European title since its last victory in 1974 in Kerpape, France. All commentators agree that the great strength of the team is the depth of its bench. Every player is able to contribute to the team's winning performance:

As a sign of this strength in depth, more players from Great Britain than any other nation, were nominated as candidates to the World all-star team which played the USA national team in Atlanta in April 1996. This match was designed to showcase the 1996 Paralympic Games. The British players were point guard STEVE CAINE, forward CALUM GORDON, shooting guard JOE JAYARATNE as well as Great Britain captain and one of the world's most dynamic shooting/point guards, COLIN PRICE. Shooting guard MARK CHEANEY was also nominated but was unable to play owing to family reasons.

G.B.'s team at Paris in 1995: (in front from left) Mark Cheaney, Colum Gordan, Colin Price (second row from left) Garry Peel, Simon Munn, Dave Bramley, Dan Johnson, Nigel Smith, Malcom Tarkenter, Steve Caine, Joe Jayaratne, Steve Owen, (third row from left) Malcom Jonas, John Stainton and Bob Dunson

OTHER MEMBERS of the World all-star team were DAVID GOULD and GERRY HEWSON of Australia, WALTER PFALLER of Austria, PHILIPPE NUTTIN of France, HIROSHI IWANO of Japan, KOEN JANSENS and GERT-JAN VAN DER LINDEN of the Netherlands and ANTONIO HENARES of Spain.

THE FINAL OF THE 1995 European Championships signals the arrival of DIEGO DE PAZ as a great player on the international stage. This is recognized as fact when DIEGO wins the MVP award.

ADDITIONAL ATLANTA men's qualification tournaments take place during 1995 and early 1996: In Amman, Jordan in August 1995, before one thousand learned and, at times, fanatical spectators, Iraq wins the one qualification place available ahead of Egypt and Jordan.

Youssri Aziz, Egypt's wheelchair basketball heart

The third qualification tournament takes place in Yamagata, Japan. Playing before 4,000 spectators, Australia beats Japan in the final game 67 v 63. DAVID GOULD of Australia, proves to the world his superstar status recording 28 points, 20 of which he scores in the second half when Japan threatens to run away with the match:

- DAVID GOULD – is Australia's greatest ever player having moved, after a shooting accident in the early 1980's, from running basketball to wheelchair basketball. In the late 1980's he played in the USA. Not of tall stature for a power forward, he possesses an incredibly high power to body weight ratio which permits him to take offensive rebounds away from taller defenders. He is always ahead of the game, both physically and mentally. In Barcelona in 1992, DAVID was the tournament's top offensive rebounder with 4.50 rebounds per match. DAVID will lead the Australian charge for gold at the 1998 Gold Cup and at the 2000 Paralympic Games, both of which are to be held in Sydney, Australia.

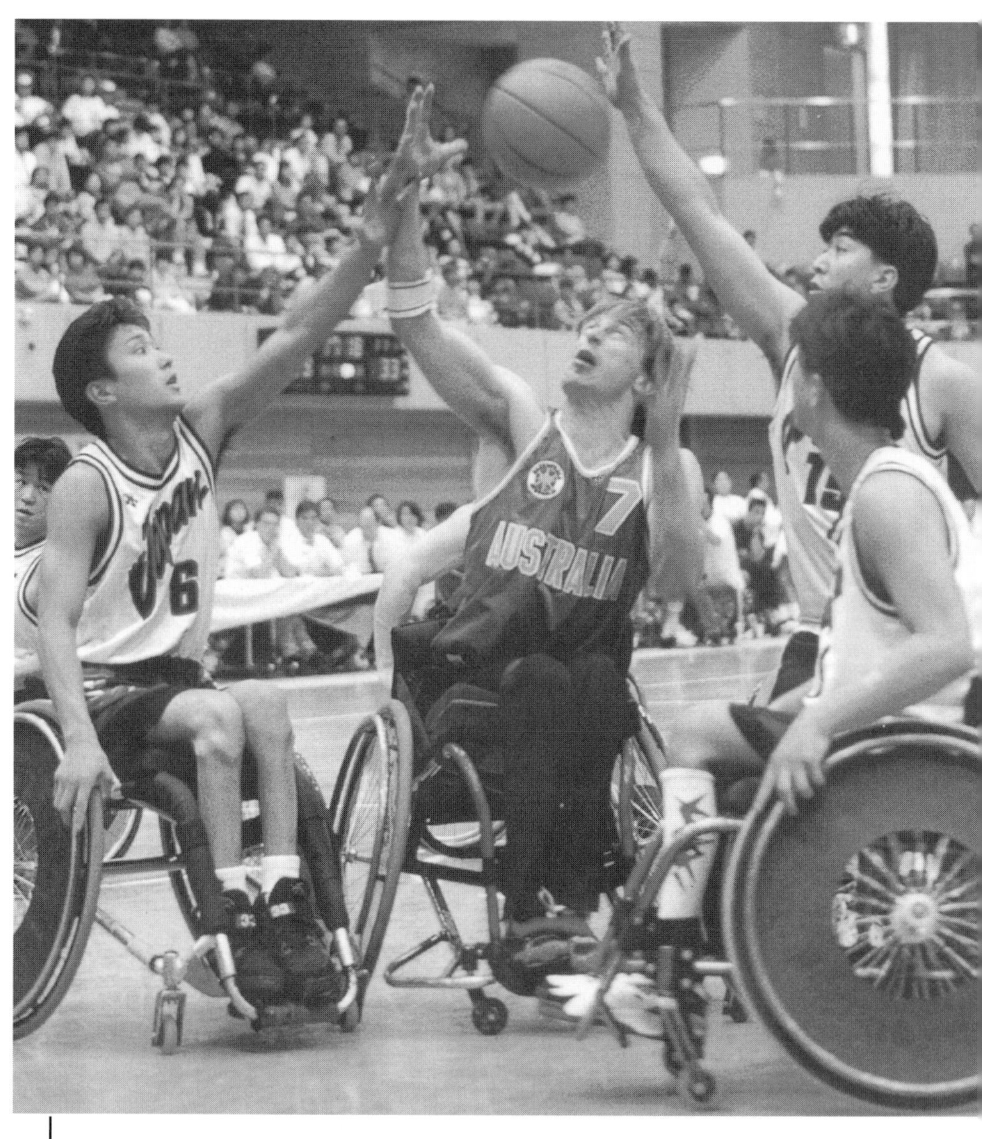

Japan v Australia at Yamagata, Japan in 1995

David Gould (No. 10)

THOUGH BEATEN IN YAMAGATA, the much improved Japanese team will be a major threat in Atlanta.

THE SIXTH WOMEN'S EUROPEAN CHAMPIONSHIP takes place in Delden, the Netherlands, in November 1995. It serves as the qualification tournament for the women's Paralympic finals in Atlanta. In a double round robin competition, the Netherlands wins Gold beating Germany in both matches by eight and six points respectively. Great Britain takes the bronze medal and the third qualification plac ahead of Israel. MARJA LEEUWEN LOKKER agai stars for the Netherlands, but Germany shows sig of regeneration under coaching duo SUSANN BAUTE and ED OWEN. HEIDI KIRSTE wins the MV award.

THE FINAL MEN'S ATLANTA QUALIFICATION tourname takes place in Buenos Aires, Argentina in Februa 1996 where Canada qualify along with Mexico an

Argentina. In the final match the highly talented, young Canadian team beats the equally talented and extremely exciting Mexican squad, 63 v 60. The Canadians have a height advantage over the Mexicans but, above all, possess two highly experienced players in ROY HENDERSON and JIM ENRIGHT who steer the Canadian young bucks to victory.

AS THE WORLD LOOKS FORWARD to tremendous basketball tournaments for men and women in Atlanta, we should all look back over the fifty years of the sport of wheelchair basketball to those early pioneers in the 1940's, without whom this great game would not have brought such competition, joy, disappointment and friendship to so many of their successors

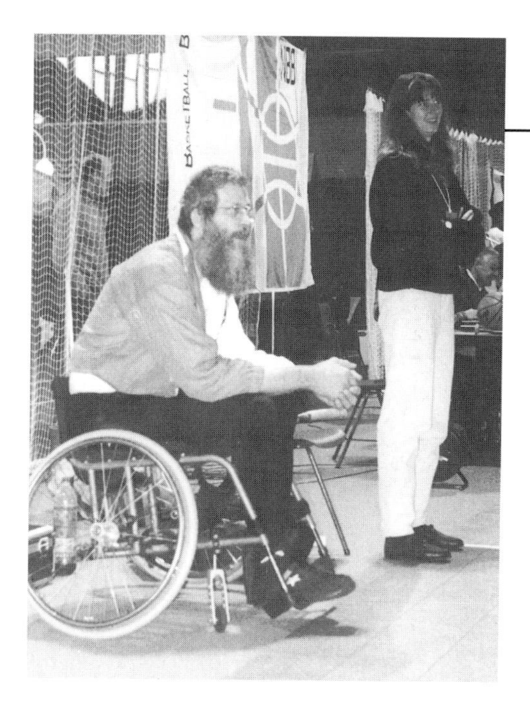

Ed Owen and Susanne Baute

Mexican's team in Buenos Aires 1996

Troy Sachs (No. 5) Australia's future; US players from left: Darran Schenebeck, Mike Schlappi and Curtis Bell

RESULTS

OF MAJOR COMPETITIONS

Paralympic Tournament/Winners

Location	Male		Female
Rome/Italy	USA	1960	
Tokyo/Japan	USA	1964	
Tel Aviv/Israel	Israel	1968	Israel
Heidelberg/Germany	USA	1972	Argentina
Toronto/Canada	USA	1976	Israel
Arnheim/Netherlands	Israel	1980	Germany
Stoke Mandeville/GB	France	1984	Germany
Seoul/Korea	USA	1988	USA
Barcelona/Spain	The Netherlands	1992	Canada
Atlanta/USA		1996	

All-Star Team: 6th Paralympiad, Arnhem, the Netherlands, 1980, from left: Sharon Rahn (USA), Rita Breuer (Germany), Rita Laux (Germany), Rach Said (Israel), Silvia Tedesco (Argentin

Gold Cup/World Championships/Winners

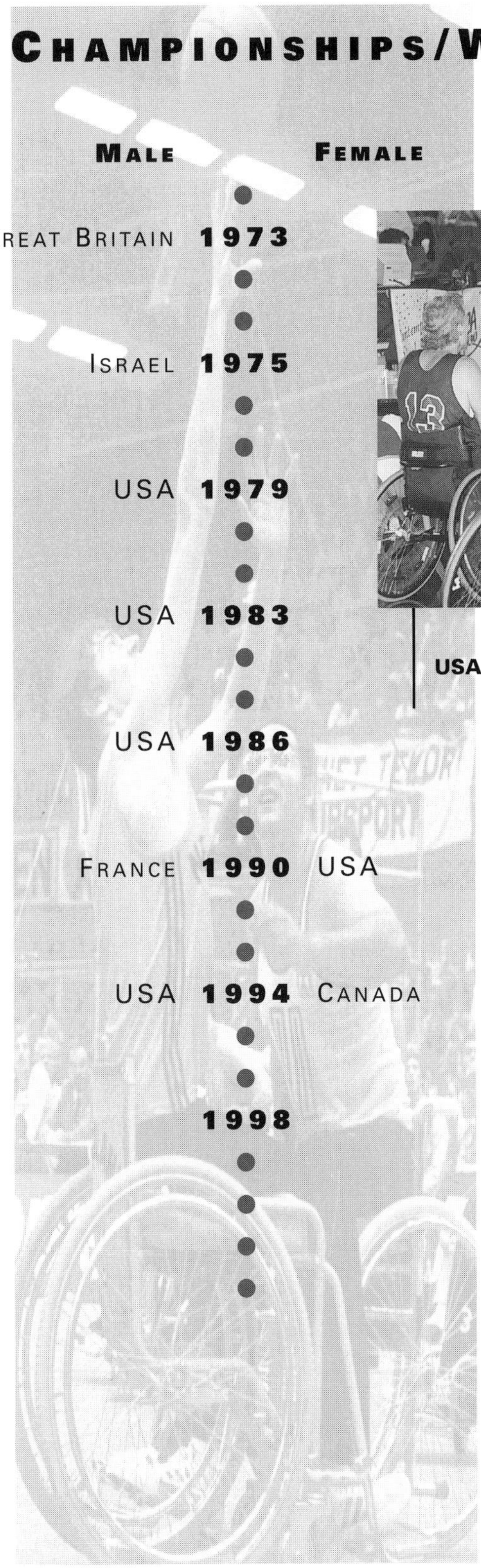

Location	Male	Year	Female	Location
Bruges/Belgium	Great Britain	1973		
Bruges/Belgium	Israel	1975		
Tampa/USA	USA	1979		
Halifax/Canada	USA	1983		
Melbourne/Australia	USA	1986		
Bruges/Belgium	France	1990	USA	St. Etienne/France
Edmonton/Canada	USA	1994	Canada	Stoke Mandeville/GB
Sydney/Australia		1998		Sydney/Australia

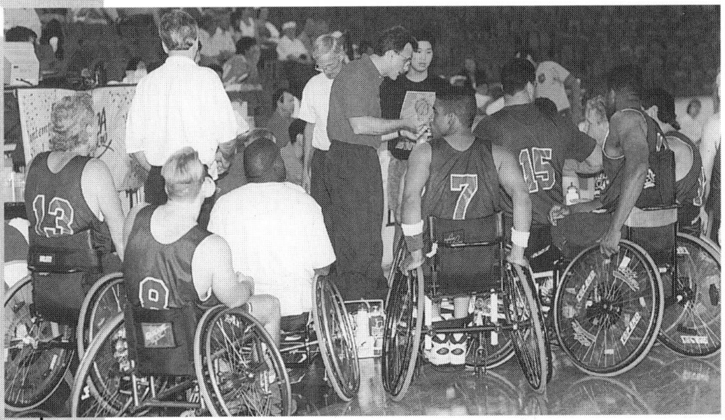

USA men's team in Edmonton, Canada 1994

European Championships/Winners

Location	Male		Female	Location
Bruges/Belgium	Belgium	1970		
Kerpape/France	Great Britain	1971		
Kerpape/France	Great Britain	1974	Germany	Kerpape/France
Raalte/the Netherlands	Israel	1977		
Lorient/France	Israel	1978		
Geneva/Switzerland	Israel	1981		
Falun/Sweden	France	1982		
Lorient/France	France	1987	Germany	Lorient/France
Charleville-M./France	France	1989	the Netherlands	Charleville-M./France
El Ferrol/Spain	France	1991	Germany	El Ferrol/Spain
Berlin/Germany	the Netherlands	1993	the Netherlands	Berlin/Germany
Paris/France	Great Britain	1995	the Netherlands	Delden/the Netherland
		1997		

Belgium's team: 1st European Champion, Bruges, Belgium 1970

European Cup Competition/Winners

Champions Cup		Andre Vergauwen Cup
I.S.A. Amsterdam/the Netherlands	1976	
SC Antilope Utrecht/the Netherlands	1977	
SC Antilope Utrecht/the Netherlands	1978	
Frisol/R Dordrecht/the Netherlands	1979	
SC Antilope Utrecht/the Netherlands	1980	
Norrbacka HIF Stockholm/Sweden	1981	
A.M.V.J Amsterdam/the Netherlands	1982	
B.V. Alsmeer/the Netherlands	1983	
B.V. Alsmeer/the Netherlands	1984	
A.S. Berck sur Mer/France	1985	
A.S. Berck sur Mer/France	1986	
Racing/R Dordrecht/the Netherlands	1987	
Racing/R Dordrecht/the Netherlands	1988	Santa Lucia Roma/Italy
A.S. Berck sur Mer/France	1989	ASPH Douai/France
Racing/R Dordrecht/the Netherlands	1990	Lodgemoor Steelers Sheffield/G.B.
BC Verkerk Zwijndrecht/the Netherlands	1991	BSG Duisburg-Bucholz/Germany
BC Verkerk Zwijndrecht/the Netherlands	1992	UBC Münster/Germany
BC Verkerk Zwijndrecht/the Netherlands	1993	IS Amsterdam/the Netherlands
Action Steelers Sheffield/G.B.	1994	US Ha Corvino Sport/Italy
BC Verkerk Zwijndrecht/the Netherlands	1995	Oldham Owls/G.B.
BC Verkerk Zwijndrecht/the Netherlands	1996	

BC Verkerk Zwijndrecht's team 1993/94

Pan American Games

Location	Male		Female	Location
Winnipeg/Canada	USA/USA*	1967		
Buenos Aires/Argentina	Argentina	1969		
Kingston/Jamaika	USA	1971		
Lima/Peru	USA	1973		
Mexico City/Mexico	Argentina	1975		
Rio de Janeiro/Brazil	Argentina	1978	Argentina	Rio de Janeiro/Brazil
Halifax/Canada	USA	1982	USA	Halifax/Canada
Puerto Rico	Argentina	1986	Argentina	Puerto Rico
Buenos Aires/Argentina	Mexico	1995	Mexico	Buenos Aires/Argentin

*Two wheelchair basketball events: 9 team balance points and 11 team balnce points.

South American Championships

Location	Winner	Year
Rio de Janeiro/Brazil	Argentina	1994
Buenos Aires/Argentina	Argentina	1996

Int. Stoke Mandeville Games/Winners

Netball Cup (1948 - 1957) **Male**

Winner	Year	
Lyme Green/G.B.	1949	
Lyme Green/G.B.	1950	
Lyme Green/G.B.	1951	
Lyme Green/G.B.	1952	
Lyme Green/G.B.	1953	
Lyme Green/G.B.	1954	
Pan Am Jets/USA	1955	
Lyme Green/G.B. (compl. l.)	1956	Pan Am Jets (incompl. l.)
	1957	The Netherlands (incompl. l.)

ISMG Wheelchair Basketball Tournaments*

Complete Lesion		Incomplete Lesion
Great Britain	**1958**	Pan Am Jets
Great Britain	**1959**	Pan Am Jets
USA	**1960**	USA
Great Britain	**1961**	USA
USA	**1962**	USA
Great Britain	**1963**	USA
Grat Britain	**1965**	USA

*Complete and incomplete lesions separated

ISMG Wheelchair Basketball Tournaments*

1st Division		2nd Division (1971-1983)
USA	1966	–
Israel	1967	–
Israel	1969	–
USA	1970	–
Israel	1971	Sweden
Argentina	1973	Canada
Argentina	1974	Belgium
Israel	1975	Spain
the Netherlands	1977	Brazil
the Netherlands	1978	Belgium
France	1979	Mexico
Israel	1981	Austria
Sweden	1982	Australia
Italy	1983	Brazil
Spain	1985	–
Australia	1986	–
USA	1987	–
France	1989	–
USA	1990	–
Canada	1991	–
Development Games	1993	–
Development Games	1994	–
Development Games	1995	–

Argentinian players

*single classification system

ISMG Wheelchair Basketball Tournaments

Female

Argentina **1970**

France **1973**

Germany **1975**

Germany **1977**

Germany **1978**

Germany **1982**

Germany **1986**

Canada **1991**

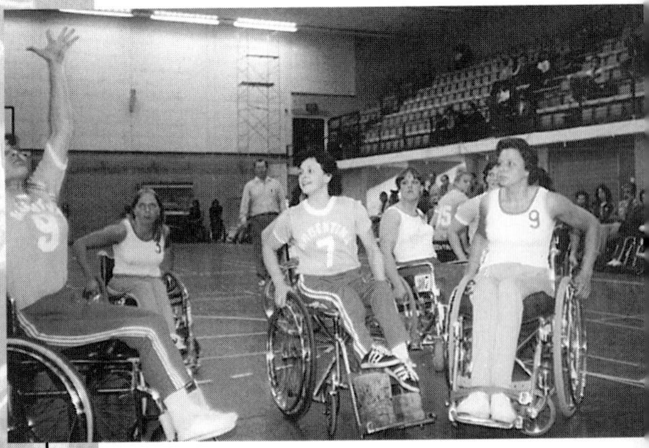

Germany v Argentina, Int. Stoke Mandeville Games 1975

5

APPENDICES

Miscallany

Eurocup for Club Teams

Founded by Hans Tukker of the Netherlands in 1975. Started as West European Wheelchair Basketball Tournament. First appointed members of the organizing committee André Vergauwen of Wapper Antwerpen, Belgium, and Willi Brinkmann of BSG Duisburg, Germany. In 1987/88 this tournament became the ► *Champions Cup* for club teams. For the runners-up in each European country, the ► *Andre Vergauwen Cup* was founded in 1988.

IWBF Logo

The IWBF logo is a heritage of the Gold Cup Organization. It was designed by Bob Deruelle, one of the first supporters of Belgium wheelchair sports, for the 1973 Gold Cup Tournament in Bruges/Belgium and awarded by the Gold Cup Committee. The original colours had been green and gold. In 1988, this logo was adopted by the IWBF with the permission of André Raes, Chairman of the Bruges' Gold Cup Committee. The colours were changed to dark blue and gold.

Gold Medal Triad Award

The Gold Medal Triad is awarded to an individual who has contributed in an outstanding manner to the growth of wheelchair basketball both on national and international level. This person must be recognized for his/her achievements by a large majority of the wheelchair basketball community. Their outstanding work serves as a model for others to follow. Outstanding contributions to wheelchair basketball can be achieved in any area of the sport: by competing as a player, by coaching, officiating, classifying, by serving at the executive and legislative level and through exceptionally effective administration and organization. The role that the award recipient played in the wheelchair basketball community should transcend personal interest and result in the betterment of the entire sport

Recipients:

1993

► *Robert Perri*

Father of the French wheelchair basketball programme and coach of the highly successful national team until 1988.

► *Henk Makkenze*

Outstanding player and leader of successful club and national teams in the Netherlands. One of the greatest point guards ever to play wheelchair basketball.

► *André Raes*

First Chairman of the Basketball Section of the ISMGF in 1973. Founder of the Gold Cup in 1973. Most efficient organizer of three Gold Cup Tournaments in Bruges/Belgium in 1973, 1975 and 1990.

1995

► *Ed Owen*

One of the game's greatest centres and allround players. International career from 1964 (Paralympics, Tokyo) until 1988 (Paralympics, Seoul/Korea) with the US team. Founder of many teams in the USA and in Germany (see Legends in wheelchair basketball). Also a great student and teacher of the game.

1996

► *Stan Labanowich*

Founding member of the Wheelchair Basketball Section of the ISMGF; Chairman of this first international organization for wheelchair basketball from 1976 - 1988.

► *Tim Nugent*

Founder of the National Wheelchair Basketball Association of the USA in 1949. Father of the philosophy of self-determination in rehabilitation and in wheelchair sports.

Pan American Games

First wheelchair multi-sports games in the Americas, founded in 1967 in Winnipeg/Canada. Allowed players other than those who were paralysed to compete on the international level in wheelchair basketball. Provided two events for wheelchair basketball: one with nine team balance-points and the other with 11 points.

South American Wheelchair Basketball Championships

First tournament took place in 1994 in Rio de Janeiro/Brazil with Argentina placing first and Brazil second. Both teams qualified for the World Championships in Edmonton/Canada in 1994.

Hans Tukker, the Netherlands
Founding member of the European Club Competitions in 1975. First President of the European Zone IWBF which was founded in 1991.

Sheila Bastos, Brazil

Founder of the South American Zone IWBF in 1993 in co-operation with Raniero Bassi.

Rizk Masri, Jordan
Founder of the IWBF Mediterranean Zone in 1993. Promoted wheelchair basketball officiating, classification and coaching in his country and in many Arabic countries.

Hamamoto Katsuyuki, Japan
First president of the Asian Zone IWBF which was founded in September 1995 on the occasion of the first Yamagata Cup.

Don Perriman, Australia
Chairman of the steering committee for the foundation of the Oceanean Zone IWBF.

Sergio Durante, Mexico
Chairman of the steering committee for the foundation of the Central American Zone.

Integration

Integration issues focus on the inclusion of wheelchair basketball into FIBA and even into the Olympic Games (LABANOWICH 1988); and eligibility of non-disabled persons to play wheelchair basketball, to compete with and against persons with permanent physical disabilities. The opinions and discussions on this issue are very controversial depending on an individual's experiences in sports in general and in wheelchair sports, as well as the prevailing cultural influences in society. The following arguments have been offered and remain under discussion:

The socio-political argument: Inclusion of able-bodied persons into the sport of wheelchair basketball can help break down barriers in communication and perception of persons with disabilities (BRASILE 1990a, 1990b, 1992; TONELLO 1991). This approach regards integration as a two-way process. BRASILE (1992) strongly recommends reverse integration, that means able-bodied persons are allowed to play wheelchair basketball in order to increase opportunities for actual integration.

The argument based on elite sport: The resolve to achieve elite performance is best realized by able-bodied persons in running basketball and by persons with permanent physical disabilities in wheelchair basketball. Able-bodied players can not reach their full athletic potential in wheelchair basketball (THIBOUTOT 1991, THIBOUTOT et al. 1992). This argument is strongly related to the philosophy of normalisation and the mutualities of running basketball and wheelchair basketball. THIBOUTOT makes a clear distinction between elite sport, recreation and rehabilitation sport. His objection related to able-bodied persons playing wheelchair basketball is solely related to competitive and elite sport.

Arguments related to sports and play theory: Wheelchair basketball uses equipment, a wheelchair, which has great impact on skill related performance and on the balance of offensive and defensive actions. The differences between wheelchair basketball and the running version are therefore not only assessed by the fact that a wheelchair player may not jump, pivot and execute lateral movements (THIBOUTOT 1991, 128) but much more by specific definitions of the rules governing Dribbling (art. 38), Progressing with the ball (art. 39) and the Personal foul (art. 47). Wheelchair basketball is not only a modification of running basketball but its own sport (RIDING 1990). A similar distinction could be seen between field hockey, ice hockey and even polo (BRASILE 1990 b, 35). Consequently, advocates of the reverse integration of able-bodied persons into wheelchair basketball maintain that this should occur because this game like ice hockey is now an independent sport.

The argument based on equal opportunity and participation: The purpose of the IWBF player classification system is to support active participation of severely disabled players. This policy includes a strong moral argument, fairness. As a result of classification, a 1-point player may not only particpate in the game on the national level, but has the opportunity to reach the highest level of international competition: World Championships and Paralympic Tournaments. It seems that the majority of IWBF members and executive make a clear distinction between national programmes and participation on the international level. Participation as an international player is a great privilege which is realized only by a small number of individuals. Able-bodied athletes possess more opportunities to qualify for international competitions than persons with physical disabilities. This is only one argument among others of a more psychological and philosophical nature which make the IWBF cautious and reluctant to alow non disabled persons to compete on the international level.

Best Teams of the USA
by Armand Tip Thiboutot

The Kansas City Pioneers won the first National Wheelchair Basketball Association's (NWBA) championship in 1949. During the next three years, the St. Louis Rams dominated the game, winning three consecutive championships. Following the 1953 championship, which was captured by the University of Illinois Gizz Kids, California gave birth to the NWBA's first dynasty, the Flying Wheels. Later known as the Long Beach Flying Wheels, this great team won seven of the next ten NWBA championships. It was led by great players such as John Cheeves, Erle Gerard and the greatest of all the Flying Wheels, Bill Johnson. Johnson, a class one player in the old NWBA system known for his passing and scoring wizardry, is to wheelchair basketball what Bob Cousy was to running basketball, the pioneer and consummate master of look-away and behind-the-back passes NWBA historian, Stan Labanowich, whose history is published in abbreviated version annually in the written programme of each NWBA championship has written: „A new power arose in 1967 in the form of the Detroit Sparks led by Bud Rumple, Denver Branum and Gary Odorowski, winning the NWBT crown in four of the next six years, and finishing second to the Illinois Gizz Kids in intermediate years.“ Rumple, in addition to establishing himself as a Hall of Fame player by virtue of his great offensive and defensive skills, designed and introduced a lighter rigid frame wheelchair to a game where players were slowed considerably by heavy, hospital-style wheelchairs. So manoeuverable was the Rumple basketball chair that, when combined with the great skills of the Detroit players, an aura of intimidation was created that often left opposing teams sensing defeat before the opening tap. The Sparks showed no mercy following the opening tap, frequently crushing their opponents by mounting scores of 100-plus points.

The Sparks won three more championships in 1977, 1979 and in 1982 after moving their home to Westland Michigan. By this time, new but comparably brilliant players such as Joe Sutika, Maurice Phillips and current international star Darryl Waller had joined the initial core of Sparks veterans. Phillips, a gifted ballhandler, astounded his fans with his sleight-of-hand, a truly ironic characterization in view of the fact that he played with several fingers missing from each hand.

Other great teams challenged the Sparks during the 1970s. Some proved successful such as the Indianapolis Mustangs who won three consecutive NWBA titles from 1973 to 1975. The Mustangs introduced Curtis Bell to the sport, arguably the most valuable player in the history of the game. Music City, the team from Nashville led by Roger Davis, an outstanding long distance shooter, was a perennial visitor to the Final Four. After winning the championship in 1966 as the Nashville Wheelcats, Music City proved victorious in 1978 and again in 1989.

Bell took his considerable talents to California and there joined forces with Dave Kiley, perhaps the most talented player to have played wheelchair basketball. The Bell and Kiley duo earned eleven Most Valuable Player awards during the years 1975 to 1992. The enviable basketball union produced the NWBA's next dynasty, the Casa Colina Condors. With Bell, Kiley and defensive stopper Al Campos, the Condors dominated the 1980s, winning six championships. They seized the first championship of the 1990s defeating the Arkansas Rollin' Razorbacks (57- 49), yet another outstanding team led by the brilliant Tim Kazee and Darren Schenebeck. Following Arkansas' triumphant climb to the NWBA summit in 1991, Casa Colina regained its championship in 1992. The next year, they succumbed to Arkansas (66 - 58), as Kazee scored a game high 32 points and won the MVP trophy as well. Arkansas and Kazee (MVP) replicated their championship performances in 1994. Arkansas won again in 1996.

Are there any potential new dynasties on the NWBA's horizon? Arkansas and Music City remain credible candidates. Add the Dallas Mavericks to that mix, ditto the Fresno Red Rollers, a finalist in 1994 and champions in 1995, after having recruited a talented and deep squad that includes all-world forward Reggie Colton. These are the teams that currently appear to have a chance at eclipsing the achievements of the Long Beach Flying Wheels, the Detroit Sparks and the Casa Colina Condors.

Best Women's Teams of the USA

by Tip Thiboutot

According to Labanowich, „A new era in the history of the National Wheelchair Basketball Association began during the 1970s when the University of Illinois Ms. Kids were established as the first women's wheelchair basketball team in the United States. The Ms. Kids built their programme from 1970-1974 by playing able-bodied opponents. On February 24, 1974, they competed in the nation's first wheelchair basketball game between two organized women's teams.“

In 1975, the Motor City Wheelers won the first national women's championship that was held in this team's home town of Detroit, Michigan. T national team from Canada captured the next tw championships in 1976 and 1977.

During subsequent years, the women's divisi would experience the total dominance of thr teams: the Southern California Sunrise, which w in 1980, 1981, 1984 and 1985 featuring playe such as Olivia Reyes and Alma Torres; as well as t game's most dominant teams, the University of I nois and the Courage Rolling Timberwolves fro Minnesota, previously known as the Rolli Gophers.

The Gophers have won six championships up 1995. They are known for their intelligent and we organized floor play and have produced outsta ding individual players such as Susan Hagel, Ma Ann O'Neil and Deb Sunderman; the latter one the best to have played the women's game.

But the most dominant team has been the Univer ty of Illinois who have won eight titles, five in su cession from 1990 to 1994. Like the Gophers, t Fighting Illni have excelled through intelligent pl and particularly through consistent picking, esp cially in the back court. A match between these tw teams inevitably produces textbook basketball. Y the University has not been lacking in great indi dual performers. Shooting guard Sharon McCart has demonstrated that by winning three MVP tr phies. Her teammate Sharon Hedrick, actually t USA's greatest wheelchair athlete, has won six, tw more than the great Sunderman.

Hall of Fame

Located in Springfield, Massachusetts, USA, t birthplace of basketball; the Hall is the panth on of basketball, honouring the greatest pl yers, coaches and organisers associated wi the game, including wheelchair basketba Great players such as Ed Owen have been gra ted a place of honour alongside legends of t running game, such as Wilt Chamberlain.

Most Valuable Player (MVP)
defines the award granted to the player who has demonstrated during the course of a game, tournament or season that his/her performance brings greatest value to the team's success.

Sportsmanship Award,
or in the USA, the Captain James Ure Award: according to Webster's dictionary: person who can take a defeat without complaint, or victory without gloating, and who treats his opponent with fairness and courtesy.

Three Second Rule
The three Second Rule was adopted by the IWBF at the World Congress in Edmonton, Canada in 1994. The delegates of the member countries of the IWBF voted to delete the former five second rule. When the ISMGF, respectively Sir Ludwig Guttmann, agreed on applying the FIBA rules as much as possible to wheelchair basketball in 1958, a player was allowed to remain six seconds in the restricted area.

Literature References

ANONYMOUS:
Londres 1957. In: Amicale Sportive des Mutiles de France. 1957, Nov. Nr. 8.

ANONYMOUS:
Runion des experts en matire de Sport pour paralyss. In: Amicale Sportive des Mutiles de France. 1958, Nov., Nr. 11.

AQSFR:
Les Wheelchair Wonders. In: A Travers les Broches, 4 (1993) 3, Fevrier/mars, pp. 12-13.

BASKETBALL SECTION ISMGF: STROHKENDL, H., RAES, L. (eds.)
Comments and Interpretations of the specific rules of wheelchair basketball. Bruges, Belgium 1982

BRASILE, F. M.:
Wheelchair sports: a new perspective on Integration. APAQ 7 (1990a) 1, pp. 3-11.

BRASILE, F. M.:
Integration through Wheelchair Sports: A Development Pespective. In: Proceedings from a national Wheelchair Basketball Symposium for Coaches, Athletes and Officials, April 25 & 26, 1990, Edmonton, Canada. CAMPBELL, B., NELSON, E. (eds.), University of Alberta: Edmonton, Canada 1990, pp. 30-39.

BRASILE, F. M.:
Performance evaluation of wheelchair athletes: More than a disability classification level issue. APAQ 7 (1990c) pp. 289- 297.

BRASILE, F. M.: Inclusion: A Developmental Perspective. A Rejoinder to „Examining the Concept of Reverse Integration“. In APAQ 9 (1992) pp 293- 304.

CLASSIFICATION COMMISSION IWBF:
Player Classification Wheelchair Basketball. Ed. by B. COURBARIAUX, Ploemeur, France 1996

CRASE, N.:
36 years of wheelchair basketball. In: Sports'n Spokes 8 (1982) 1, May/June, pp. 10-11.

CRAVEN, P. L.: The development from a medical classification to a player classification in wheelchair basketball. In: DOLL,-TEPPER, G., DAHMS, C., DOLL, B. & VAN SELZAM, H. (eds.), APA : Proceedings of the 7th International Symposium. Berlin, June 1989. New York: Springer 1990, pp. 81- 86.

CURTIS, K. A.:
Wheelchair sportsmedicine. Part. 1: basics of exercise physiology. In: Sports'n Spokes 7 (1981) 1, May June, pp. 26-28.

CURTIS, K. A.:
Wheelchair sportsmedicine. Part 2: training. In: Sports'n Spokes 7 (1981) 2, Juli/August, pp. 16-19.

CURTIS, K. A.:
Wheelchair sportmedicin. Part 3: stretching routines. In. Sports'n Spokes 7 (1981) 3 Sept/Oct, pp. 16-18.

CURTIS, K. A.:
Wheelchair sportsmedicine part 4: athletic injuries. In Sports'n Spokes 7 (1982) 5, Jan/Feb, pp. 20-24.

FEDERATION FRANCAISE HANDISPORT (ed.):
Le basketball en fauteuil roulant. Boulogne Billancourt, France 1984

GUTTMANN, L.:
Textbook of Sports for the Disabled. Aylesbury/England: HM & M Publishers 1976

HEDRICK, B., BYRNES, D. & SHAVER, L.:
Wheelchair Basketball. 2nd edition, Washington: PVA 1994

HEDRICK, B.:
Women's wheelchair basketball: a perspective on the US program. In: Sports'n Spokes 11 (1985) 4, Nov/Dec, pp. 14-17.

HEDRICK, B., HEDRICK, S.:
Women's wheelchair basketball. In HULT, J.S. & TREKELL, M. (eds.), A century of women's basketball: from frailty to final four, Reston, v.a., American Alliance for Health, Physical Education, Recreation and Dance, 1991, pp. 367-378.

HUBERMAN G.:
17th International Stoke Mandeville Games in Israel, Results. Tel Aviv/Israel 1968

IWBF:
Constitution and Internal Regulations. Ed. by L., RAES, Bruges, Belgium 1995

IWBF:
Official Wheelchair Basketball Rules, as adopted by the 1994 World Congress. Ed. by L., RAES, Bruges, Belgium 1995

LABANOWICH, S.:
Wheelchair Basketball: A History of the National Association and an Analysis of the Structure and Organization of Teams. Doctoral Dissertation, University of Illinois at Champaign 1975

LABANOWICH, S.:
The Physically Disabled in Sports. Tracing the influence of two tracks of a common move-

ment. Sports'n Spokes 13 (1987) 6, March/April pp. 33-42.

LABANOWICH, S.:
Wheelchair Basketball Classification: National and International Perspectives. Palestra 4 (1988a) May/June pp. 14-15; 38-40 & 54.

LABANOWICH, S.:
A Case for the Integration of the Disabled into the Olympic Games. In: APAQ 5 (1988b) pp. 264- 272.

LABANOWICH, S., THIBOUTOT, A.:
Wheelchair Basketball: The International Story. In: Proceedings from The Second International Wheelchair Basketball Symposium for Coaches, Athletes and Officials, March 29 & 30, 1991, Toronto, Canada. NELSON, E., HOLLAND, L. (eds.), University of Alberta: Edmonton, Canada 1991, pp. 47-61.

LYKINS, R.:
Recruiting for Wheelchair Basketball. In: Proceedings from The Second International Wheelchair Basketball Symposium for Coaches, Athletes and Officials, March 29 & 30, 1991, Toronto, Canada. NELSON, E., HOLLANG, L. (eds.), University of Alberta: Edmonton, Canada 1991, pp. 89-94.

McCANN, C.B.:
Classification Guide for the use of doctors, sec. Draft July 1975. ISMGF (ed.) Stoke Mandeville/England 1975

NUGENT, T., J.:
Let's look beyond the treatment center, our professional disciplines, our categorical concepts and limitations on disability; to put meaning to recreation in treatment centers. In: Recreation in Treatment & Centers 3 (1964) pp. 33-42.

OWEN, E.:
Playing and Coaching Wheelchair Basketball. Champaign, USA: University Press 1982

RIDING, M.:
Functional Classification in Wheelchair Basketball. In: Proceedings from a National Wheelchair Basketball Symposium for Coaches, Athlets and Officials, April 25 & 26, Edmonton, Canada. CAMPBELL, B., NELSON, E. (eds.), University of Alberta: Edmonton, Canada 1990, pp. 63-66.

SCHWEIKERT; H.S., Jr.:
Sports Highlights. In: Paraplegia News 3 (1949) Nr. 19.

Schweikert H. S., Jr.:
A History of Wheelchair Basketball. In: Paraplegia News 8 (1954) Nr. 18.

SCRUTON, J.:
History of the ISMGF and its relationship to other intern. organisations. In: ISMGF Symposium: Ludwig Guttmann Centre for the Disabled. 27th July 1985. Aylesbury/Engl. 1985, part two.

SHAVER, L.:
Wheelchair Basketball: Concepts & techniques, Marshal, Minnesata: Southwest State University 1981

STROHKENDL, H.: Zur Problematik der Schadensklassifizierung im Wettkampfsport der Rollstuhlfahrer unter besonderer Berücksichtigung des Basketballspiels. In: DECKER W. (ed.), Kölner Beiträge zur Sportwiss. Bd.2, Schorndorf: Hofmann 1974, pp. 272-288.

STROHKENDL, H.:
Funktionelle Klassifizierung für den Rollstuhlsport. Springer: Berlin, Heidelberg, New York 1978.

STROHKENDL, H.:
Classification System for Wheelchair Basketball. In: Basketball Section ISMGF, Handbook 1984-1988, pp. 13-15.

STROHKENDL, H.:
Functional Classification and Self-determination of Athletes in Wheelchair Sports. In: ISMGF Symposium: Ludwig Guttmann Centre for the Disabled. 27th July 1985. Aylesbury/England 1985, part four.

STROHKENDL, H., OTTO, W.:
Curriculum Referees Training for Wheelchair Basketball. Bonn/Germany 1988

STROHKENDL, H.:
Implications for Understanding and future Development of the sportspecific Functional Classification in Wheelchair Sports. In: ISMWSF, Proceedings of Kevin Betts Sports Science Symposium on Functional Classification. Held on 23rd and 29th July 1991 at Postgraduate Medical Centre Auditorium Stoke Mandeville Hospital. Aylesbury/England 1991

STROHKENDL, H.:
Development of the German female Wheelchair Basketball. In European Zone IWBF (ed.) Newsletter 1994, 1.

SZYMAN, R.: Goin' for the Gold in '84. In: Sports'n Spokes 8 (1982) 1, May/June, pp 25-28.

TECHNICAL COMMISSION, IWBF:
Handbook, Section III. Bruges/Belgium 1991

TECHNICAL COMMISSION, IWBF:
Positioning in Wheelchair Basketball. Bruges, Belgium 1995

THIBOUTOT, A.:
Classification, time for change. In: Sports'n Spokes 12 (1986) 2, July/August pp. 42-44.

THIBOUTOT, A., CURTIS K.A.:
NWBA Classification: The Player, Coach and Classifier Perspectives. In: Sports'n Spokes 16 (1990) 1, May/June, pp. 46-47.

THIBOUTOT, A.:
Able-Bodied Involvement in Wheelchair Basketball. In: Proceedings from The Second International Wheelchair Basketball Symposium for Coaches, Athletes and Officials, March 29 & 30, Toronto, Canada. NELSON, E. HOLLAND, L. (eds.), University of Alberta Edmonton, Canada 1991, pp. 119-129.

THIBOUTOT, A., Labanowich S. & Smith R.W.:
Examining the Concept of Reverse Integration A Response to Brasile's „New Perspective" on Integration. In APAQ 9 (1992) pp. 283-292.

THIBOUTOT, A.:
US Veterans beat Celtics... back in 1946. In NWBA Newsletter 1995, p. 14.

TONELLO, J.:

Playing Wheelchair Basketball: An Able Bodied Perspective. In: Proceedings from The Second International Wheelchair Basketball Symposium for Coaches, Athletes and Officials, March 29 & 30, 1991, Toronto, Canada. NELSON, E., HOLLAND, L. (eds.), University of Alberta: Edmonton, Canada 1991, pp. 131-134.

'ORTH, J.:
Certified & qualified: are they really equal? A noted wheelchair basketball player comments on an alarming trend in the quality of wheelchair basketball officiating. In: Sports'n Spokes 12 (1986) 1, May/June, pp. 56-58.

ANLANDEWIJK, Y.C., SPAEPEN, A.J. & LYSENS, R.J.:
Relationship Between the Level of Physical Impairment and Sports Performance in Elite Wheelchair Basketball Athletes. In: APAQ 12 (1995) pp. 139-150.

Photographic References

age	name/resource/additional information
. 5	U.M.A., Arnhem, the Netherlands from left: Frits Streyl, Baruch Hagai (Israel), Frits Wiegmann
.12	A.T. Thiboutot
.13	above/Sports'n Spokes
.13	below left/A.T. Tiboutot
.13	below right/S. Labanowich
.14	CWSA (Canadian Wheelchair Sports Association)
.15	above/T. Nugent
.15	below/Sports'n Spokes
.16	ISMWSF (International Stoke Mandeville Wheelchair Sports Federation)
.16	ISMWSF
.16	ISMWSF
.16	ISMWSF
.16	ISMWSF
.17	above/ISMWSF
.17	below/ISMWSF
.18	above/ISMWSF
p.18	below/K. Hamamoto, Japan
p.19	left /Don Perriman, Australia
p.19	right/A. Raes, Belgium
p.19	above/A. Raes, Belgium
p.20	above/A. Raes, Belgium
p.20	below/S. Labaonowich
p.20	right/H. Strohkendl
p.22	above/CWS from left: Murray Brown, Bill Inkater, Ron Minor, Phil Allan (coach), Rick Hansen with Peter Colistro, Chris Sobkowitz, John Stubbert, Frank Henderson, Dean Mellway, Roy Brideau, Dave Rudderham, Reg McClellan
p.22	below/CWSA
p.23	below/D. Perriman
p.23	above/P. Craven
p.24	left H. Strohkendl
p.24	right/J. Berteling
p.24	middle/H. Strohkendl
p.25	above left/B. Courbariaux
p.25	below left/H. Strohkendl
p.25	below middle/R. McClellan
p.25	below right/K. Curtis
p.25	above right/R. Moreno
p.25	right middle/CWSA
p.28	left /ISMWSF
p.28	right/R. Heller/Intergraph., Israel
p.29	CWSA
p.30	left/M. Dekel, Israel
p.30	right/K. Curtis
p.31	left /R. Heller
p.31	right /U. Ehlich, Germany
p.31	above/Delfina Colby, Sports'n Spokes
p.32	left /Sports'n Spokes
p.32	right/Sports'n Spokes
p.32	above right/Shoko Kitamura, Japan
p.32	below right/Shoko Kitamura, Japan
p.33	above left/Sports'n Spokes
p.33	below left/Sports'n Spokes
p.33	middle/DRS
p.33	above right/DRS
p.33	below right/CWSA
p.34	above left/Jürgen Morich, Germany German's national team in 1988, from left: Rita Breuer, Heidi Kirste, Anja Happel, Corina Robitschko, Nu Nguyen-Thi, Rita Laux, Karin Leybold, Britt Tuna, Nadira Mazri, Michaela Richter, Liesel Bröckerhoff, Angelika Gerstmeier, standing: Hans Groll (coach), Ilka Nowottny (physio), Malik Abes (manager), Dieter Joswig, (technician), Hans-Jürgen Völpel (M.D.), Monika Motyl (ass. coach)
p.34	centre/CWSA 1st row from left: Irene Wownuk, Kendra Omaha, Marni Abbott, Jennifer Krempien, Diane Rakiecki, Helene Simard; 2nd row fr. left: Linda Kutrowski, Petti Jones, Judy Goodrich, Judy Millard, Tracy Ferguson, Chantal Benoit; behind from left: 4th Barb Griffin, 5th Joe Higgins, 6th Tim Frick
p.34	below right/CWSA
p.34	below middle/CWSA
p.35	left /CWSA
p.35	right/D. Perriman, Australia
p.35	right middle/R. Masri, Jordan
p.35	below/Eric Brinkhorst, the Netherlands
p.38	left/CWSA
p.38	right/ISMWSF
p.39	left /K. Hamamoto, Japan
p.39	right/E. Brinkhorst, the Netherlands
p.40	H. Strohkendl
p.41	H. Strohkendl
p.43	left /H. Strohkendl
p.43	below middle/T. Barnett, England
p.43	right/K. Hamamoto
p.44	above/G. Vera, Spain
p.44	left /CWSA
p.44	right/Argentinian Federation on Sport for the Disabled
p.44	below/Shoko Kitamura, Japan
p.45	T. Barnett, England
p.47	below left/H. Strohkendl, classifiers in South America, from left: Eduardo de Garay Vasquez (Mexico), Sheila Salgado

(Brazil) and Luis Paz (Argentina)
p.51 E. Schropp, Germany
from left: Theel Wolfram, Bornschlegel Ludwig, Siemund Werner, Müller Karl-Heinz, Altenburg Günter, Schropp Erich, (missing Bosch Rainer, Fuchs Richard)
p.52 left /Sports'n Spokes, R. Smith
p.52 right/B. Courbariaux
p.53 right/H. Strohkendl
1st row from left: Posse Frederico, Rawahi Al Mukhtar Mohamed; 2nd row from left: Don Perriman, Strohkendl Horst, Garrett Jeffrey, B. Courbariaux, Dinh Tan Trien, Sheila Bastos Salgado
p.56 Peter van der Velde, the Netherlands
p.58 above/Sports'n Spokes
p. 58 below/ISMWSF
p.59 above/P. Craven
p.59 below left/T. Nugent
p.59 below right/T. Nugent
p.60 left /P. Craven
p.60 right/CWSA
p.61 CWSA
p.62 Cynthia Johnson, USA
p.63 left /Cynthia Johnson, USA
p.63 right/D. Perriman
from left: Allan Yeomans, Ivan Watts, Robin Lucas, Kevin Coombs, Bruno Moretti; standing: Fred Martin (coach), Pat Carney (referee).
p.64 above left/Sports'n Spokes
p.64 below right/Intergraph, Israel
p.64 above right/R. Heller, Israel
p.65 below/I. Freidin, Israel
p.65 above/R. Laux, Germany
p.66 Sports'n Spokes
p.67 left /R. Heller, Israel
p.67 centre/R. Heller, Israel
p.67 right/R. Heller, Israel
Israel's national team in 1982, from left to right: Gaziel Zvi, Levi Moshe (No. 7), Yacov Zion (No. 6), Carmeli Shmuel (No. 4) Vagima Shaul (No. 13), Momo Nakeva (No. 3), Shafran Yoel (No. 8), Caim Cohen (No. 14), Shaban Shachkapi (no. 9), Hagai Baruch (No. 11), Amoyel Yossi (No. 12), Rubin Arie (No. 10), standing: Shelach Shimon, Heller Reuven
p.67 above right/Sports'n Spokes
p.68 above/R. Verheuvel, the Netherlands
p.68 below/P. Craven
p.69 above/P. Craven
p.69 below/P. Craven
p.70 above left/R.Heller, Israel
p.70 below left /P. Craven
p.70 above right/P. Craven
p.70 below right/R. Laux
p.71 above/Gray Garner, England
p.71 below/Sports'n Spokes, C. Beamer, USA
p.72 above/R. Heller, Israel
p.72 below/Sports'n Spokes, C. Beamer, USA
p.73 above/P. van der Velde, the Netherlands
p.73 right/R. Verheuvel. the Netherlands
p.74 left /Sports'n Spokes
p.74 right/E, Benault, France
p.75 left /DRS (German Wheelchair Sports Federation)
p.75 right/CWSA
USA team 1986 from left: Bruce Karr (manager), Randy Snow, Rickie Helms, David Kiley, Albert Campos, Curtis Bell, Kevin Lowrie (No, 14), Robert Murdock, Joseph Manni, Joe Sutika
p.76 /Sports'n Spokes, C. Beamer, USA
p.77 left /P. Craven
p.77 middle/E. Benault, France
p.77 right/CWSA
p.78 centre/Sports'n Spokes
p.78 above right/Sports'n Spokes
p.78 below right/Sports'n Spokes, C. Beamer, USA
p.79 above/DRS
1st row from left: Norbert Weinrauter, Lisa Goede, Paul Kühnreich, Günter Ritter, Holger Glinicki, Stefan Donner; 2nd row: Georg Beschler, Wolfgang Schäfer, Rainer Schumacher, Frank Michael, Bertl Schauberger, Adi Wiesnet; standing: Friedhelm Köhn, Wolfgang Raabe, Ulf Mehrens (coach)
p.79 left /D. Krings, Germany
p.79 centre/Horst Schure, Germany
p.79 right/L. Friar, England
p.80 left /Sports'n Spokes
p.80 right /DRS
p.81 above/P. Craven
French team at Bruges in 1990, 1st row from left: Maurice Schoenacker (coach), Jean-Jaques Reignier, Jario Fahrasmane, Lionel Chavanne, Jean-Denis Aboukir, Michel Gradelle, Michel Mensch, escort; 2nd row from left: Jean-Luc Genete, Alain Kiefer, Eric Benault, Philippe Nuttin, Jean Yves Regnault, Jean-Louis Granzotto; 3rd row from left: Bernard Ganser, Daniel Starck, Claude Benderitter, Michel Paul.
p.81 below/ Sports'n Spokes
p.82 above/The Netherlands men's team at Assen in 1990, 1st row from left: Peter-Brandsen, Bob van den Broek, Gert-Jan van der Linden, Rene Martens, Anton de Roy, Servaas Kamerling; 2nd row from left Frans van Breugel, Rob Verheuvel (coach), Edward d'Hooghe, Waldo Boonacker, Ben Klerks, Wilbert Cappetijn, Frits Wiegmann.
p.82 left/R. Verheuvel, the Netherlands
p.82 right/H. Strohkendl
p.83 left /CWSA
p.83 right/E. Brinkhurst, the Netherlands
p.84 above left/Sander Faassen, the Netherlands
p.84 below/Servaas Kamerling, the Netherlands
p.84 above right/K. Hamamoto, Japan
p.85 left/P. Craven
p.85 centre/Sports'n Spokes
p.85 right/Sports'n Spokes
p.86 above/P. Craven
p.86 centre/H. Strohkendl
p.86 below/D. Perriman, Australia

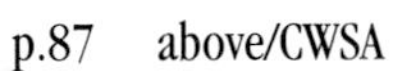

p.87 above/CWSA
p.87 left /G. Garner, England
p.87 right/W. Pfaller, Austria
p.88 left /R. Coppenrath, the Netherlands
p.88 middle/P. Craven
p.88 right/R. Coppenrath, the Netherlands
p.89 above/P. Craven
p.89 below/H. Strohkendl
p.90 right/K. Hamamoto, Japan
Japan v Australia at Yamagata in 1995, from left: Karetomo Keisuke, Miyake Katsumi (No. 6), Blythe Sandy (No. 7), Oushima Tomohiko (No. 15), and Mitzumoto Eiki (No. 7).
p.90 left /D. Perriman, Australia
No. 10 David Gould, No. 4 Sandy Blythe and No. 9 Michael McFawn
p.91 below/P. Craven
p.91 above/Gregor Pleßmann, Germany
p.91 above right/Argentinian Fed.
p.94 R. Laux, Germany
p. 95 Sports'n Spokes
p.96 A. Raes, Belgium
Belgium's national team in 1970, 1st row fr. left: Jacky Meeus, Aime Desal, Frank Jespers, Gerard Delobel, Marc Deboel, André Allemersch, Roger Meulemeester, Daniel Vanbelleghem; 2nd row from left: Marcel Ornelis (coach), Michel van Maele (mayor of Bruges), André Raes (organizer), Bob Deruelle (President SV St.-Jan)
p.97 Sander Faassen, the Netherlands
from left: Jef v. Loon, René Martens, Wilbert Cappetijn, Sander Markus, Van Nelisen, Gert-Jan van der Linden, Servaas Kamerling, Anton de Roy
p.101 Peter v. d. Velde, the Netherlands, from left: Guillermo Prieto, (No. 11), Argentina, Frits Streyl (No. 8), the Netherlands, Hector Leurino (No. 6), Argentina
p.113 H. Strohkendl
p.115 T. Nugent

IWBF Excecutive Committee

1st row from left: Raniero Bassi (Brazil), Reg McClellan (Canada), Philip Craven (GB), Armand „Tip" Thiboutot (USA); 2nd row from left: Ricardo Moreno (Spain), Horst Strohkendl (Germany), Rizk Masri (Jordan), Kathleen Curtis (USA), Luc Raes (Belgium), Jan Berteling (the Netherlands), Hans Tukker (the Netherlands), Bernard Courbariaux (France)

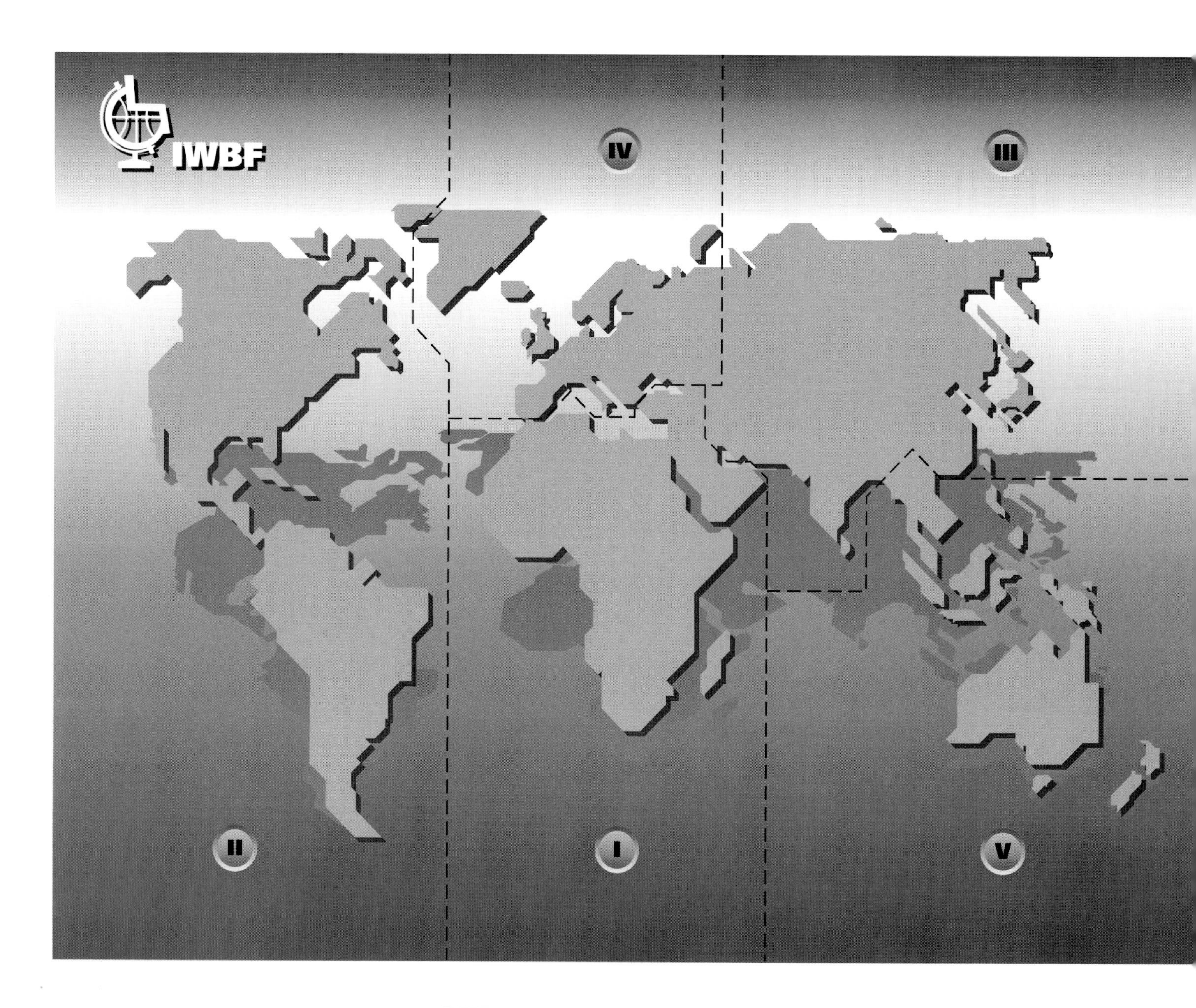

IWBF Zones

I - African/Arab Zone
II - American Zone
III - Asian Zone
IV - European Zone
V - South East Asian & Oceanian Zone

IWBF Zones

I – African/Arab Zone
Algeria, Angola, Bahrain, Burkina Faso, Cameroon, Egypt, Guinea, Iraq, Jordan, Kenya, Kuwait, Lebanon, Libya, Mauritania, Marocco, Nigeria, Sultanate of Oman, Palestina, Saudi Arabia, South Africa, Syria, United Arab Emirates, Zimbabwe

II – American Zone
Argentina, Brazil, Canada, Bolivia, Chile, Colombia, Costa Rica, Cuba, El Salvador, Jamaica, Mexico, Nicaragua, Panama, Peru, Puerto Rico, Uruguay, USA, Venezuela

III – Asian Zone
People's Republik of China, Republic of China, Hong Kong, I.R. Iran, Japan, South Korea, Sri Lanka

IV – European Zone
Austria, Belgium, Bulgaria, Croatia, Cyprus, The Czech Republik, Denmark, Estonia, Finland, France, Germany, Great Britain, Greece, Hungary, Iceland, Ireland, Israel, Italy, Lithuania, Luxemburg, The Netherlands, Poland, Portugal, Russia, Slovakia, Slovenia, Spain, Sweden, Switzerland, Turkey

V – South East Asian & Oceanian Zone
Australia, Indonesia, Malaysia, New Zealand, Singapore, Thailand

Tim Nugent in 1996
Recipient of the Gold Medal Triad Award of the IWBF on the occasion of the 10th Paralympiad in Atlanta, USA